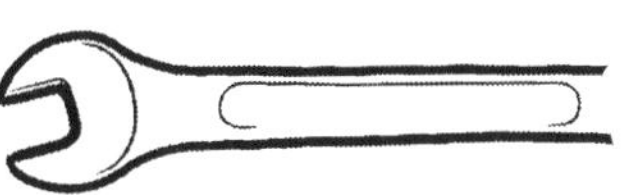

In memory of my father, Leigh, whc
how to make, my own way, while makir

NICK BOWMAST'S

USERPALOOZA

A FIELD RESEARCHER'S GUIDE

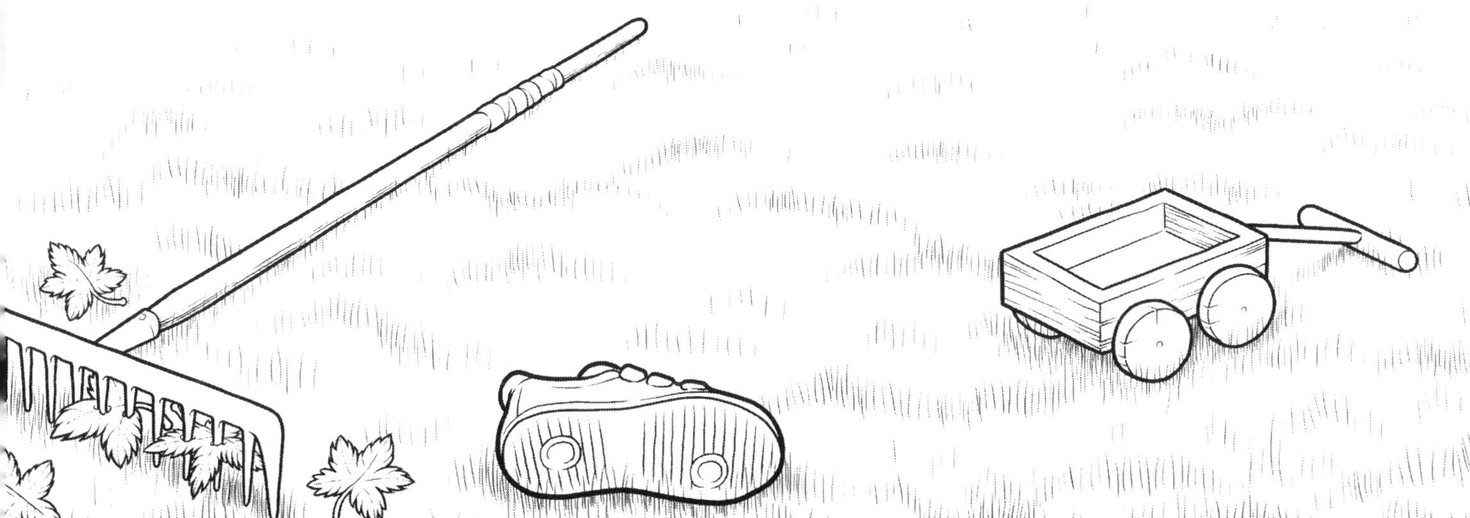

... because it's easier to design for a customer you understand.

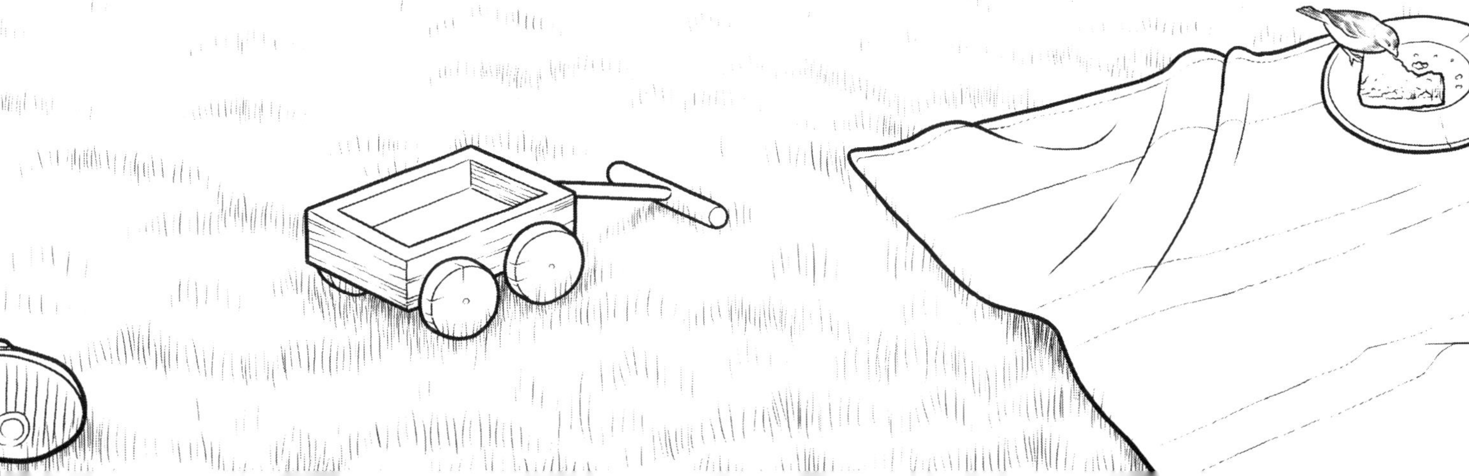

USERPALOOZA – A Field Researcher's Guide

ISBN: 978-0-473-45876-8

Enquiries to: nick@bowmast.com

Illustrations: Mat Tait

Editor: Jude Watson

Layout and graphics: Nick Bowmast

0. HELLO

Shaped by curiosity

For fifteen years while working in industrial, architectural and digital design, I conducted what I now know to be field research, in order to understand my customers. Learning how a product might fit their world made the brief clearer, and my job easier as a result.

Nobody told me this was research, but it felt better putting something out into the world understanding what really mattered to the end-user of the product, and that it would more likely hit the mark. For example,

- in the surf industry, when champion surfers asked me to shape and build their next board, I went surfing with them to find out how they rode.
- in architecture, when property clients asked me to design living/working-space apartments, I visited people who already worked from home, to see how they had found that balance within their space.
- when website clients asked me to design their online presence, I asked to meet their customers first.

I've since spent about the same amount of time working as a design researcher, focused on understanding who to build the design for and why, rather than what to build and how. I help design, product and marketing teams define their brief, bringing the voice of the customer into their work.

This fascinating work has taken me through beauty spas and abattoirs, grocery stores and factory floors, high streets and edit suites, and through thousands of homes, to understand people's needs in their contexts. With no guidebook or formal training to rest on, I've relied on an empathy for the designer's position, and loads of curiosity. It's addictive and I love my work.

So, why userpalooza?

Today's brands aspire to be user-centred. They talk of 'putting the customer at the centre of everything we do'. That's fine if you're on the front line of sales, but for those who work in design or marketing, the first step is to do the opposite. You need to put yourself at the centre of everything the customer does. Physically. Literally.

This involves field research, to understand who your customer is, how they think and what they do. Teams want to learn these skills, but too often are as unfamiliar with their customers and their worlds as they are with ways to research them.

What's more, they're in a hurry, operating in 'sprint' cycles, adopting a 'pedal-to-the-metal' pace of product development. These research approaches might add some value but usually only scratch the surface in terms of insight, while introducing bad habits.

Teams therefore get a taste for the value of what can be learned by spending time in their customer's world, but their approach is more user-scented than centred.

I wrote this book to help people in those teams. For those who want to meet and understand the people they're designing for, to bring their voices, experiences and realities to bear on the way a brand brings its product or service into the world.

The book also scratches my own itch. Much of the content was written directly for my clients who I often need to coach – not to become experts, but to understand how to think about this work, and the basic approaches when visiting customers in their context.

I've been converting what I've learned organically through experience into a body of material to prime clients/teams before taking them into the field or before letting them loose to make their own discoveries. These pages are the product of some of that material.

The depth I choose to go into in each section reflects the areas in which my clients have needed the most guidance or asked the most questions about. The sections provide the grounding for how to think about each phase of a fieldwork project, and they offer practical advice for how to get the most out of it.

I've enjoyed shaping my experience into this format. I hope it helps you discover what matters to your customer, so you can use this to inform how you design for them.

1. INTRO

Never assume?

Quite the irony to begin this book with the very thing it's sent to kill.

So for the first, and last, time in these pages, here's a hefty assumption:

I figure you appreciate and believe understanding your customer and their context through research is a strong foundation on which to make informed design decisions. You've been part of it. Perhaps it's become part of you and the way you work.

Either way, you want it to be part of the way you develop products and services.

I make this assumption because I'm not here to 'sell' benefits or list case studies and success stories – I'm here to help you get even more value from design research, and make it count.

This book also assumes you've experienced a few 'a-ha' moments and a few 'oh shit' moments too. You've realised – with research – 'you get more out than you put in', and you're wanting to put more in.

If I've assumed right, keep reading.

This book is for you if...

- you want to understand your customer - for yourself, your clients or your internal teams.
- you work in the trenches of brand, marketing, or design - physical or digital - and want to understand how people think, feel and behave around your product or service.
- your team or clients are insight-starved and looking to fuel their decisions about what really matters to customers, by meeting them in their world.

What you'll learn.

How to think about, plan and conduct successful field research to inform design projects.

How to gain insight and understanding by connecting with your customer, either visiting them in their home or context.

- Who to talk to, how to choose and find them
- Priming yourself and your team for a high value immersive experience
- Capturing moments that matter with notes, images and audio
- Interview techniques and tools to open your senses and your customers' world
- Making sense of your data
- Shaping and sharing your insights for engaging, lasting impact.

Field focus.

USERPALOOZA covers initial planning and in-field activity with more detail than later analysis and synthesis. This follows my experience - that a team who 'sweats the details' early is more likely to do the analysis justice and communicate and stand by their findings, because they've invested and believe in the way the data was collected.

The rise of design...

Appetite for design as a professional skillset and organisational mindset has never been stronger, and never been more human.

From things we tap and click to changes in how governments tick, design is seen as an essential ingredient in the generation and delivery of successful products and services.

Design thinking can take a gracious curtsy for its role in fuelling this demand, with packaged activities providing corporate exposure to many facets of design – most notably research and prototyping.

‘Sprints’ and ‘hack-days’ promote design as an intensive bootcamp-style activity, like adopting a crash diet where you’re guaranteed to lose, or rather, emerge as a winner with a validated product and a business model to support it.

At the start line of all variants of the human-centred design process lies the necessity to understand people, to define their needs, attitudes and motivations. A key message is to ‘get out of the building’ and into their lives. This means research, specifically fieldwork.

It’s encouraging to see organisations investing in this: learning about, from and with their customers.

... but, too often teams accelerate to the horizon in a storm of sticky notes. They rush through activities – sometimes called ‘empathy’ – without realising how fundamental to strategy is a nuanced and considered understanding of their customer.

...Informed by research

Some way into their 'honeymoon' with design, teams realise they're relying on instinct rather than insights.

Their experience of being introduced to design research has been streamlined down to bite-sized chunks. This suited the short timeframe and 'learning by doing' philosophy, but speed has come at the cost of quality and rigour.

They need to loop back; they may wish they'd dug a little deeper or for longer, delving into the lives of people, markets or contexts.

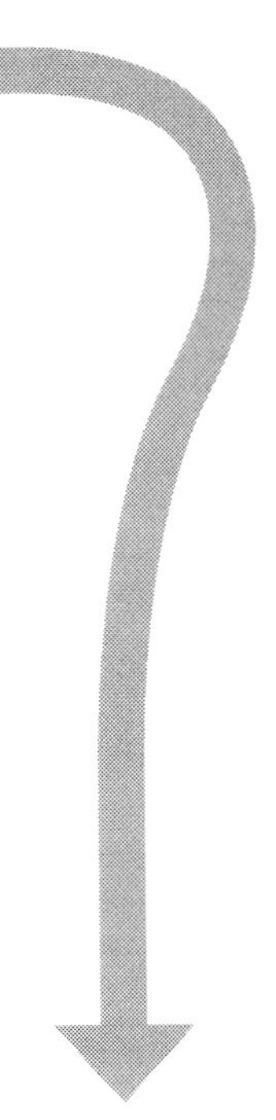

Dig deeper

This book aims to help those who want to go deeper with design research.

With your curiosity as your spade, let the following pages help you find out where and how to dig, and how to share the insights for maximum impact.

2. RULES OF ENGAGEMENT

Things to know before you go

Make change

Beyond uncovering truths, decoding behaviour, discovering opportunities, inspiring and informing decisions, the role of design research is to drive change.

This may be change in the way the customer is viewed, how the problem space is defined, the way the product is communicated, and ultimately, material change in the product or service itself.

Before even half a degree of change hits home in one of these areas, though, there's a long-standing challenge to be overcome: changing peoples' mindsets, as individuals and as a collective culture. Make this your target, but don't expect to bullseye too soon.

There are forces at play ...

EGO ASSUMPTION
EXPERTISE BIAS
RISK STATUS QUO

EVIDENCE STORY
TRUTH EMOTION
CHANGE INSIGHT

Know your enemies

Design, intentional or not, by process or proxy, is going to happen on your project. It's happened on every project and with every product. Ever.

However, research to inform the design often has a corner to fight. Weighing in at 300lb is the main opponent – ego: a person's self-belief and need to be right. Other more organisational opponents are bias and assumption. Entrenched and unquestioned beliefs around how customers behave or think, and the 'we've always done it that way' status quo.

You might have checked all of these at the door, but part of your job is to encourage others to do the same – to reframe their default perspectives.

It takes humility for a decision maker to admit there's a gap in their understanding, especially if they feel like they're the one in the room who should have the answers.

You'll need to be ready to have your diplomacy tested, should your insights be seen as a threat to those who are experts on the market, category, subject matter, etc.

Research is associated with risk, too. The project sponsor might use research to reduce risk, but others in the organisation might see it as a risk to the progression of the project. (I've had research insights trigger major rethinks, and even kill projects.)

It may seem the odds aren't great, given the opposition, and that we're measured by the degree to which we make change. But with the invitation comes an obligation: to challenge perceptions, reveal truth and meaning from ambiguity and find answers to better questions.

Curiosity first...

Empathy is the first step in the classic 'design thinking' framework and often portrayed as the vital ingredient in innovation.

But while fully appreciating your customer's worldview is essential in design research, you can't simply 'magic up' empathy by getting out with a notepad. Empathy is something you invest in. It's an outcome, not a tool or an approach. You need to earn it, through applying deep curiosity and social skills.

If empathy is something you need to work to gain, it seems curiosity is a challenge to retain. We're all born with an enquiring mind, but as we gain life experience it can be superseded by pesky things like education, knowledge and a sense of risk.

For some people, though, curiosity never fades, making aspects of life endlessly fascinating. The tendency to question and the desire to understand – thoughts of 'How does that work?'; 'What's actually going on here?'; 'Could there be a better way?' play as a backing track to their experiences of life – almost to the point of becoming a burdensome curse.

If I've just described you, welcome to the club. Like me, you probably pulled apart your toys to find out how they worked.

Many designers and researchers share this curse and have found research to be a satisfying outlet for their curiosity. They've made a career out of pulling things apart, but in this case the toys are products, businesses and people. It's when you apply your curiosity to people that empathy emerges.

Not everyone in the project will share the same levels of curiosity, so for product or marketing teams whose curiosity about their customer has faded, it's a researcher's duty to draw out the client's business questions, embedding these into your own mindset.

...empathy later

I like to believe by absorbing (and amplifying) these questions, your curiosity can become contagious and can infect the team through a kind of osmosis – by reflecting these unknowns back, by visualising, reframing and refining them with the team. It can make gaps in understanding tangible, and the team accountable for addressing them, or at least in them agreeing on what the research needs to achieve.

If by advocating for enquiry you can re-build this curiosity among the team, their empathy should follow. There's no guarantee you'll succeed, but one usually follows the other.

It's about people

All too easily we talk about 'customer segments', 'early adopters' or 'target markets', but this language can mask what really matters.

These collective labels act as a smoke screen, putting distance between the people designing and those who will ultimately use the product.

Seeing past these labels to the person means letting individuals' glorious differences and similarities shine through, rather than treating them as segments or personas.

Encourage your team to view the wider context of people's lives and to understand where a product or service can add value to a person.

'Talking about users, it lets you imagine that the only moment that matters is the moment someone is encountering the thing you have built, but the reality is, human beings exist in a myriad of circumstances beyond the point they intersect with your thing, and if we're not paying attention to all of that we miss things.

There's an industry shorthand – talking about users and user experience, but if it's not ultimately grounded in an idea about humanity and people, you make stuff that doesn't matter, or you make stuff that doesn't work.'

Genevieve Bell, anthropologist

Embrace the unknown

Being comfortable with chaos is a blessing in design research.

It can save you drowning in the depths of customer insights. And if you'd rather drown in a pie, then make it a humble one, because when you're involved in design research, you need to be content with not knowing answers to the questions you've been asked. For days on end.

It takes personal and corporate courage to let go of this sense of security; to embrace the unknown and learn to swim in the ambiguity.

Heavy lifting

If you dig deep enough - even on a seemingly mundane topic - there is always emotion.

I've had people drawn to tears in interviews about mortgages or nutrition. As people reveal their experiences, these stories can pull on your heart strings, bring up to the surface philosophical thoughts, moral and sometimes ethical dilemmas.

There's a reason this is often referred to as 'deep dive' research. That's what it can take to uncover invaluable insights.

Soaking in other people's emotion can be an occupational hazard for design research, and where emotion is involved, if you're not being affected, then you're probably not going deep enough.

Respect

A personal relationship can be measured by how close we get to people. As we become closer and more comfortable, we share more, and with our closest friends, we'll reveal our vulnerabilities. This quality of connection is something we earn and value in a relationship.

However, in a transactional relationship, such as with a market stall-holder you might see most weeks, the parameters and social boundaries of the relationship are well-defined norms.

You might never drop your guard, reveal your insecurities ... and you'll likely never say they are 'close'... unless you cross that boundary and invite them for dinner.

A field visit to a participant's space lies squarely in the transactional (you're usually paying them for their time) but it depends on your ability to create the level of trust and intimacy required to cross that boundary into 'close'.

If you're doing your job well, you'll give a stranger the permission and safety to share about things that have meaning or which are a part of who they are.

And then you'll be gone.

This will happen more in some product and service categories than others, and some conversations just won't go that deep. But when we enter a private space and a person gives much more than their time, revealing concerns, sharing personal anecdotes and giving us a window into their lives, it's a privilege.

Honour this. Be respectful in your behaviour, from removing your shoes on arrival to finishing on time, and everything in between. Maintain their anonymity, and take on the mantle of representing their needs throughout the project.

Safety

Design research comes with its share of hazards.

Fieldwork is not always conducted in the confines of your own stomping ground.

To include a diversity of, or a specific type of participant you're often in unfamiliar territory – any mixture of physical, conversational, social, cultural or emotional.

Pushing through comfort zones can become part of the job.

While some uncomfortable encounters can be brushed off with humour and notched up to experience, there are some that stay with you long afterwards.

Project goals are important, but make sure looking after yourself and your team is one of them.

A good start is to follow these rules of thumb ...

Take a buddy

Having a partner in the field is a solid rule of thumb, not just for safety, but the quality and impact of your work.

On a practical level, having a dedicated note-taker allows the lead researcher to be more present and focus on the conversation.

There's nothing like knowing your partner has 'got your back' especially when it comes to judging an uncomfortable situation, and debriefing after an unusual encounter.

If your partner/note-taker is a client the immersion and exposure in their customer's world can be an invaluable eye opener, contributing to a culture of being customer-centred and building appetite for more research or more focused research.

Operating in pairs works both ways. Let participants know it's fine for another person to be with them during the session, even if they don't contribute.

Check in

Share your appointment schedule with someone back at the office, let them know when you check-in/out of a session.

If on approach to a property you're feeling unsure for any reason, phone the participant to come out to get you or 'talk you in' as you navigate to the entrance. I've even asked a participant to walk me back to my car.

Bail-out

There are comfort zones, then there is risk. If you're approaching an address and your instinct tells you it's the latter, don't ignore it.

From your perceptions outside or inside the property, or in the way a participant behaves, don't hesitate to pull out. No fact-finding, product development or marketing challenge is worth risking your personal safety.

Alibi

Agree on a 'code phrase' to use as a signal when either of you feel it's time to end a session early, like 'the camera is malfunctioning, looks like we'll need to reschedule'.

Avoid

Report difficult participants to your recruiter. If *you* didn't feel comfortable, neither will the next researcher.

Download

On projects with emotionally taxing subjects or people in vulnerable positions, absorbing the reality of people's stories can become overwhelming. Build in time to unload and recover. Counsellors and therapists call this 'transference' and schedule regular sessions to unload in order to stay professionally effective.

An alternative to paying someone to listen is to find a friend or someone on your project team to talk to (always being mindful of respecting privacy/anonymity of the participants).

3. PLANNING

The key to confidence in your outcome

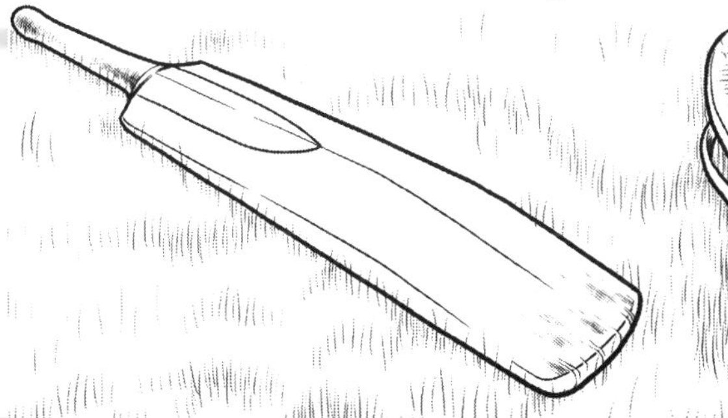
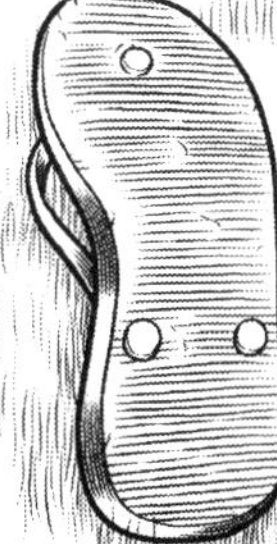

Checklist

Time spent planning will reward you right through the project.

From the start – with consensus among your team around project goals.

In the field – by being in the right place at the right time

During a visit – with the reassurance your camera won't max out of storage.

but, most importantly ...

At the end – with confidence you spent time well, with the right people, leading to credible, evidence-backed findings your team can rely on.

Objectives:
Research questions, hunches & hypotheses.

People:
Participants. A carefully selected sample of participants to visit.
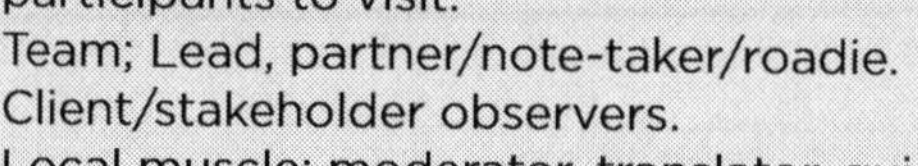
Team; Lead, partner/note-taker/roadie.
Client/stakeholder observers.
Local muscle; moderator, translator, guide etc. (If in another language)

Admin & logistics:
Schedule of who, where and when to visit.

Paperwork; Agreements, permissions etc.
Cash/gifts to say thank you to participants.

Materials:
Prototypes, games, artefacts for people to respond to.

Kit:
Recording gear; eyes/ears, cameras, audio, video, notebook.

Chargers, media, batteries.

Mindset:
Curious, open, determined, respectful, gracious.

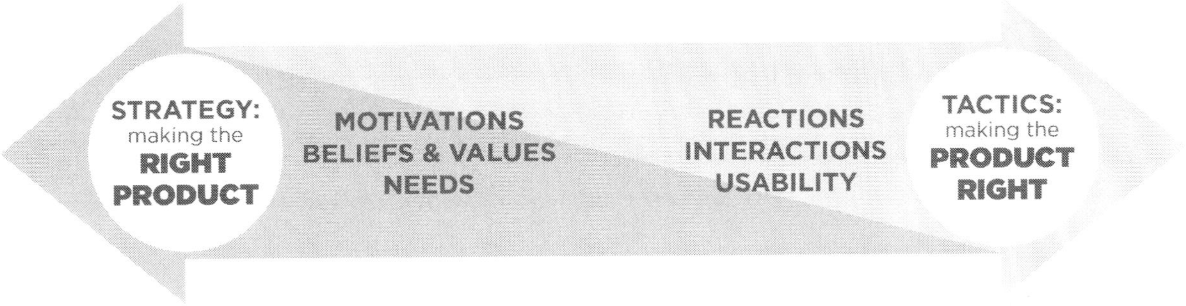

STRATEGY: making the **RIGHT PRODUCT**

MOTIVATIONS
BELIEFS & VALUES
NEEDS

REACTIONS
INTERACTIONS
USABILITY

TACTICS: making the **PRODUCT RIGHT**

Explore ▶ Evolve ▶ Evaluate

Research in product development runs along a spectrum from strategic and generative through to more tactical, evaluative work; from 'making the right product' to 'making the product right'. This can also be viewed as defining the problem, through to designing the solution.

Fieldwork is best employed, and most valuable, at the front end of this spectrum, when it's sometimes referred to as 'discovery phase' design research. Insights gained early and upfront reflect peoples' needs, often fundamental truths with enduring shelf life, informing design or experience principles that the product is built upon, remaining relevant for the duration of a project and beyond.

Fieldwork is also essential because 'making the wrong product well' happens all too often.

As a project moves along the spectrum, other design research activities come into their own:

- co-design activities - generating concepts with your customers
- user testing - evaluating a prototype through a user's point of view for usability, fine-tuning of messaging, etc.

What you learn here will be directly translatable into tactical improvements to the product, such as validating which features have the most value to customers.

... but you want to be sure to be solving the right problem, before solving it well.

Shaping your brief

Be confident of the problem you're solving before you rush into ideas and ways to solve it.

The same applies when beginning a research project, but rather than defining a 'problem', it's the project objectives that you need to clarify and agree on, with the people who are going to value the insights most.

This is a critical investment. The success of any project hinges on how well you elicit, understand and respond to this brief.

Because we often don't yet know what we need to learn, we need to be explicit about what we do know, what is assumed, and what the hunches are.

We'll need to know the background, too:

- What data or evidence are the hunches and hypotheses based on?
- What design or business decisions does the team need to make, based on the outcomes of the research?
- Why is now the right time to conduct this research?
- How will the business measure market success for the product/service?

You'll need to know the areas in which the team feels confident they have sufficient insights. For example, a mobile-device maker told me they explain to all their researchers, *'just don't make your key insight be "people want longer battery life - We're investing millions into this already"*.

Knowing this is covered means that when this issue comes up in interviews, the team can move right along into more fertile ground to get maximum value from each session.

Then it's down to the 'brass tacks' of the brief. And there is no such thing as being too specific here.

Say you're working with a car manufacturer. They're wanting insights about the car-buying process from the customer's point of view.

You'll need to glean from them exactly which aspects they are interested in, so you can build your approach to best answer the brief.

Possible areas might be:

- what triggers the need for a new car?
- how does a buyer do research?
- how does a buyer interact with dealers?
- what is the decision-making process?
- what influences a buyer's decision?

Defining the scope of questions now, and knowing why the answers are important, will help you provide sharper, more useful insights later. This is scoping, and you owe it to your team/ client to nail this down. In fact, you can't progress in good faith without it.

A thorough brief will help inform the entire approach: the sample of car buyers, the research method/tools, where and when in the buying process you meet the participants, the boundaries of your conversation with them, and perhaps of dealers, too.

So - when it comes to taking the brief, don't be brief.

But do work with the client to be concise.

Hunches & Hypotheses

Behind many design research projects lies a hunch or vision for a product or service that may exist in the future.

Bringing the hunch to life as a prototype introduces a great learning opportunity, giving people something tangible to respond to, boosting the relevance and value of your insights to the design challenge ahead.

Market researchers would call this 'stimulus material' and it's worth taking a creative and deliberate approach to what aspect is most likely to stimulate the answers you need.

A prototype could be anything from a paragraph of text describing the concept, to a working model, or even a competitor's product. I'll always lean towards a prototype that allows people to imagine themselves interacting with the product, but which lets them decide what the benefits will be, rather than responding to a sales pitch of features or ideas they might think you're wedded to.

Being careful about what you include and what you leave out of the picture helps you make the most of the participants' contributions to the research. Sometimes it's better to hold back on the detail, leaving room for interpretation rather than presenting fixed ideas.

Always hold off from showing your prototype until you've gained a clear picture of your participant's world, their attitudes and behaviour. This provides a vital frame of reference, allowing you to sense-check their response.

EXAMPLE:

BREW YOUR OWN PROTOTYPE

When a home-brew company wanted to launch a new system aimed at craft beer brewers, we spent time in basements and garages to observe their current process, then showed our prototype.

Rather than wowing with shiny stainless steel components, we mocked up a one-page 'quick start guide'.

Being intentionally brief in our descriptions left room for brewers to project their mental model onto the concept, revealing aspects where messaging was vital to their grasping the process - aspects we may have missed if we'd fleshed them out according to our own assumptions.

PEOPLE

Who's in?

The old saying 'Garbage in, garbage out' applies when considering a sample of people to meet in the field.

Your sample will be a small number of people who contribute significant 'per capita' impact to your project, so you'll need to carefully consider who the sample will consist of.

Quantitative research tools like data-analytics and surveys go wide, relying on numbers for their outcomes. This type of data can show us the what, when, who, and how many. But it doesn't show the 'why'.

To get to the why, design research takes a qualitative approach. It's not about the number of participants or being a representative sample of the market, it's about going narrow and deep, including people selected for the dimensions and attributes we can learn the most from.

You'll kick yourself later if you rush this. So will your client. They'll poke the sceptic stick at your sample for not being representative or statistically valid enough, saying, 'you didn't include any type X customer'.

If they don't have confidence in your sample, they won't have confidence in your insights.

Build this confidence upfront by treating this as a conversation – a collaborative journey you'll need to navigate with your client team until they understand the rationale behind the criteria for who's in and who's out of your sample.

Working through this process, you'll also learn more about your team's knowledge gaps, assumptions and biases around who their customer is.

In this section I'll explain how to shape your sample of people, then find them, using a professional people-finder known as a recruiter.

How many people? It depends

Sample size is usually a reflection of your market and/or research question, specifically, how broad or narrowly defined these are.

If you have a very focused question aimed at a narrow target market, it'll be a low number. If it's a broad question and a wide market with many segments, you'll need to head north with your numbers.

EXAMPLES:

To learn about how teenagers with type-2 diabetes manage their diet, your learnings might peak after a handful of participants.

To learn how people plan their holidays, you'll need to go broader to accommodate different types of people and different motivations, contexts etc. As you tighten up your criteria, such as 'how do families with pets plan their holidays', you can confidently reduce the sample size.

As a rough guide, five people would be a minimum for a targeted study, while 25–30 is a comfortable maximum when there's a need to go wide. Above this the sheer quantity of information becomes unwieldy and is likely to be repetitive.

If a client asks for 30 or more in a sample, options are to grow the team then divide & conquer, or to suggest starting with a smaller number, then running a second more-targeted study once it's clearer where you need to be looking.

Just past saturation

You'll know when you hit this point – when you're no longer learning anything new from each participant. It's a sign you're either not digging deep enough or you've reached 'peak a-ha'.

Aim for just beyond this point.

Life's a beach

How small can be beautiful

It's hard to defend using a small sample against a sceptical data junkie, but get used to explaining how less can be more.
A market researcher once gave me this analogy and I've not bettered it yet:

If you wanted to understand all the grains of sand at the beach, it would be a painstaking task, and probably not suited to everyone.

But, if, with a few pointers from a beach-ologist, you took a pinch of each from: high-, middle- and low-tide zones; near the rocks; by the boat ramp; where the sunbathers gather; and that area by the old wharf where the seaweed washes up after a storm.

With only a sprinkle of sand in total, there's a fair chance that you'd actually covered it. You'd also be able to highlight and associate the differences between the grains from their various locations.

It's likely you would need to go back to one or two areas to dig deeper, but this could be done with purpose.

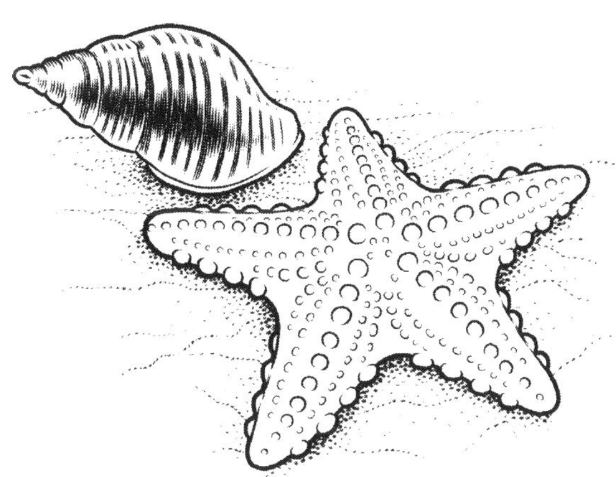

Double down

A way to boost the sample size without blowing out on time-in-field or reaching data saturation is to recruit pairs. The dynamics you can observe between two people adds depth and is worth considering, in many contexts.

EXAMPLE:

DISCOVERING THE POWER OF PAIRS

While learning how they navigated a cable TV on-demand product, kids were arriving, chaperoned by their parents or grandparents. The moment when a 12-year-old patiently talked his grandpa through the user-interface was priceless.

The value, for this researcher, was in the natural, unedited dialogue – uncovering the child's mental model as well as seeing grandpa's sense of discovery at the use of buttons and controls he'd never thought to use.

Sometimes you need to manage the share of 'airtime' between the two participants, but you can reveal contrasts in attitudes, experiences and behaviours while observing people interacting with an object, or demonstrating to each other how they use something.

A pair might also keep each other honest. I've seen mates 'call bullshit' on each other – an 'Oh come on, when was the last time you did that?!' response. At this point, they're doing my job for me; the dynamic between them presenting a reality that may not have surfaced in a one-on-one.

Knowing they're keeping each other honest means you can pick up on subtler social cues between them, such as body language. A sideways glance with a raised eyebrow from one friend to another while they explain something can be a strong tell there's more to the story, and your opportunity to play devil's advocate.

When?

Timing is important where a customer experience plays out over time or when there's a 'relationship' between the customer and the product/service.

In an ideal world you'd connect with the same participants through different phases, as they navigate interactions, to compare expectations and realities of their experience along this timeline.

This is not always practical, so you can find yourself talking to separate people in each of these phases and interpolating.

EXAMPLE:

To understand the end-to-end surgery experience in a hospital, I interviewed patients in the Emergency Department, then on the ward pre- and post-op, then in their homes after being discharged.

This approach allowed us to experience some of these moments with them, gauging their expectations and reflections at each stage.

Picking your moment can help in other ways, too. If you wanted to understand (and reduce) customer churn in a subscription product, for example, you'd want to meet lapsed customers to try and understand why they stopped using the product, what triggered them to bail out, and what are they using now?

Representative versus revealing

If you're running a 1000-person survey it makes sense for the shape of your sample to be representative of your market, but for a qualitative study with perhaps a dozen or so participants, you want to be sure they are representative of the challenges your customers present, rather than being an accurate slice through the bell curve.

To test your product's pulling power, the sample should have people on the edges - and even fleeing. Their attitudes to your product will help turn up the contrast, and maybe even push you in new directions.

Look to the edges

A common oversight in user-research recruiting is to avoid 'rejectors' of a product or service. The thinking goes something like: 'If they'd never use the product, what could we learn from them?'

This attitude stems from product teams seeking validation. In their desire to hear 'good news' about their idea they'll go after easy-to-recruit advocates (usually by mining their social media followers).

Everyone loves good news but, what are they missing out on?

EXAMPLE:

GET OUT OF THE BIKE LANE

If you're researching for the design of a bike-sharing scheme and only talk to people who currently ride or drivers open to the idea of bike-sharing, you're missing out.

Get out of the bike lane. Talk to that woman who used to ride but now has a raft of reasons why she'll never ride a bike in the city again.

This woman would be classed as a 'rejector' and would be 'screened out' of most samples, but people like her need to be included. They provide vital contrast and perspective; a new lens through which to view your product - challenging its place in the market.

Alternative viewpoints help define who your core customers are, what matters to them, and how your product meets their needs. And because great products and services convert people to the value they offer, make sure you're testing the 'pull' of your proposition by including the people who might be the hardest to convert.

Which customers are you talking to?

When defining a sample, marketing teams sometimes refer to a bell or adoption curve. As it's difficult to place where these 'hard-to-reach-but-worth-the-effort' types live on the curve, I use this version, a bird's-eye view of the bell curve.

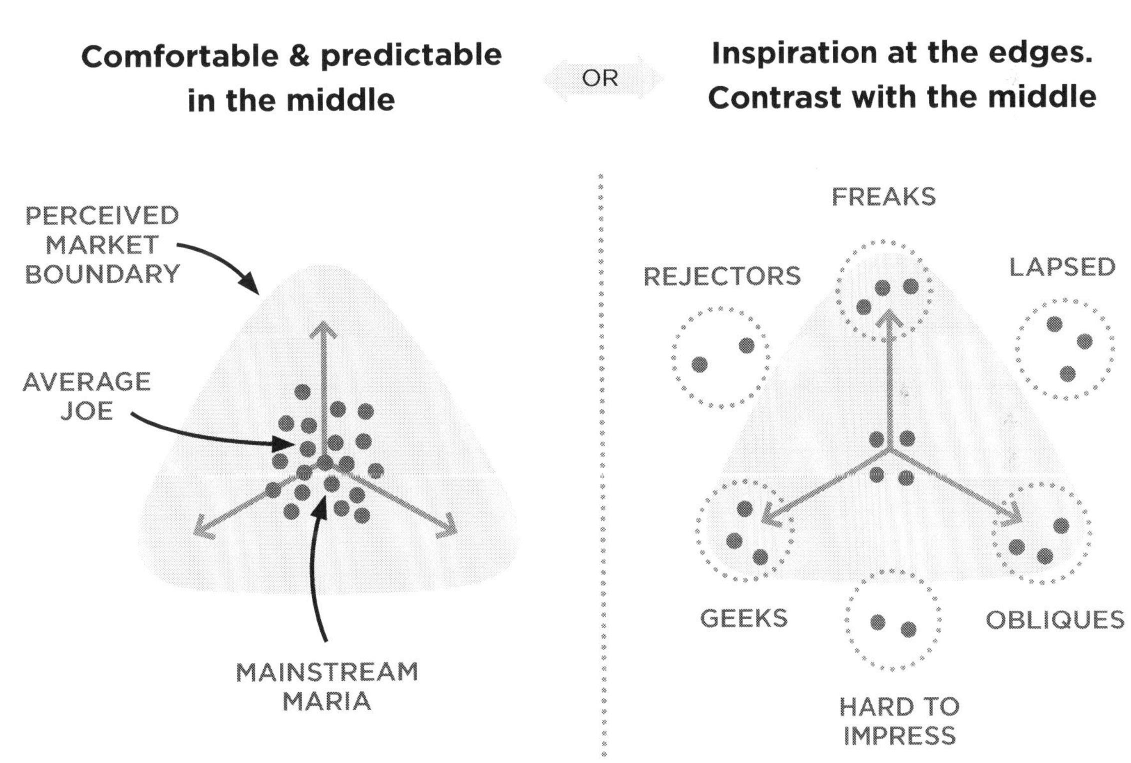

Professional recruiters

If you're going to invest in spending time with customers or potential customers, using a professional qualitative research recruiter is a great way to go.

How recruiters work

Recruiting can be a stand-alone service or one offered by market research companies. When a food brand wants school kids to taste and rate some new flavours of yoghurt, or a political party wants to test straplines for a new campaign with the voting public, they can use a recruiter to find the kids and the voters.

It's a professional skillset, and recruiters have many tools in their arsenal. Their 'big gun' is often a whopping, and well-tagged, database of thousands of consumers, as well as some software to sort the wheat from the chaff. They keep their databases up-to-date, continually learning about the individuals by surveying them regarding many aspects of their lifestyles. This means you can be fairly specific in the level of detail in your sample.

BYO customer list?

If you're able to provide a list of customers/followers/subscribers who have consented to be contacted, this can be a great start. Hand this to your recruiter to build into their workflow. They'll run a survey to 'screen-in' the type of people you're interested in, and politely tag and release the remainder.

Creative approaches

Recruiters can be as creative as they are charming. To find needles in human haystacks, they'll go to where the people are most likely to be.

If the project is about how people choose accessories for their mountain bike, they'll reach out to a downhill-riders forum.
I heard of a project requiring owners of overweight dogs. The recruiters headed to the beach at sunrise, where they found their owners ~~dragging~~ walking them.

When I needed people who had recently moved into a new home, off they went door-knocking in a sparkling new subdivision.

When you find a recruiter like this, stick with them.

Deep connections

Some recruiters have networks in certain communities as a result of doing work in a specific product category, so it can pay to ask upfront about a recruiter's area of strength. While one might shine finding surgeons, another may be well connected to horse riders or home-improvement fanatics.

Recruiters typically estimate and charge for how long it takes to find each participant, so it makes sense to work with one who's preferably not starting from a zero base.

Needles in a human haystack

EXAMPLE:

TRACK & FIELDWORK

A fitness-tracking device maker wants to investigate wellness during business travel. Their hunch from anecdotal evidence - business travellers struggle to maintain their exercise routine while on the road.

They want to understand this type of customer to validate the opportunity and learn what their needs are.

You ask the recruiter to find you 15 frequent business travellers to be interviewed in their home or workplace:

- to travel for business twice monthly
- to be located across two cities
- to exercise at least twice a week
- for half to belong to a gym
- for 10 of them to use any type of fitness tracking device
- for 5 of them to use your specific brand of device
- for visits to happen at their place of work for half of the sample
- to be available during specific dates

The recruiters can quickly assess their database, narrowing thousands down to hundreds of people who meet the easiest criteria: location and perhaps business travellers. Then an email is sent out, with a multi-choice survey to check; frequency of travel, whether they belong to a gym, do they have a device and if so what type? They might even ask them whether they'll be around during the target dates. Before long responses from likely candidates start arriving back into the system.

From here, recruiters use an army of 'charmers', with their phone list and a set of carefully sequenced 'screener' questions, to phone, assess and charm potential participants, lining up the most suitable to take part. They are also experts at 'blinding' the questions in their screener, so people can't guess the type of person they're looking for and just say what they think the recruiter wants to hear.

Targets and tradeoffs

At various stages in this process, a recruiter may need to check with you regarding the mix. Questions like:

We've got plenty of people with the fitness device, but only some of them actually use it. Is that OK?

It's hard to find people who will say yes to meeting at their work. If we only had five at work, is that OK?

We only need one more gym member.
We're talking to one who meets all the criteria, and actually works in a gym as a trainer, but she doesn't travel much for work.
Shall we keep trying for a traveller or will she be OK?

These questions help, because some of what the recruiter discovers might force you to relax the criteria. Other times you'll need them to keep pushing.

Assess the trade-offs of missing one criterion to hit another.
What's the minimum number of at-work visits you're comfortable with? Could you meet them at a cafe near their work? Is the fact she works in the fitness industry going to help or hinder?

The more specific you can be upfront about what an ideal set of people for your sample will be, the easier it will make the job for your recruiter, and the more likely you'll get what you want. But be prepared for the realities of the world not to reflect your 'idealised' sample. Be prepared, and make sure your client/team is flexible.

Briefing a recruiter

A recruiter works to a specification. They have the criteria (attributes of types of people) and quotas (how many of each). They're used to working to a defined target and you'll typically need to show them what the bulls-eye looks like, so don't hold back on the specifics.

A recruiter looks at the desired criteria amongst the sample and aims to reach maximums and minimums of each: three of these, four of those, at least 30 per cent in this life-stage, etc.

EXAMPLE:

HOME BUYERS
A project for a bank around home buying with a sample of 18 people

Start by describing the criteria you DO want in your sample and how many of each you'd like:

- Individuals or couples who have recently bought or are in the process of buying a house
- A mortgage from a mix of banks (at least five banked with the client)
- Age range: 25–70 with at least ten between 35 and 50
- Life stage: a mix of singles, young couples, families with baby/toddlers/teens, empty-nesters
- Buyer types: mixture of first-time buyers, young families, upsizing families, downsizing retirees and buy-to-let investors
- Five interviews to be with couples, the remainder with individuals (who may or may not have bought as a couple)

You'll also need to think about who you DON'T want in your sample:

- A spectator in the buying process, where a partner has done the legwork
- A home buyer six months or later since buying. All to be in the middle of the home-buying process or have recently gone through the process (<3 months ideal; <6 months ok only if able to recollect details)
- None to have, for example, bought their brother's place and not looked at other options etc. All to have experienced the process of searching for a home to buy
- None to work in, be closely related to, or living with people who work in the real estate or mortgaging industries

All of this will come together as a specification for the recruiter. They will aim, but won't guarantee, to deliver on it exactly, but you can help them get closer by providing the rationale behind your decisions to bias in one direction or the other.

Enough, already?

This may all seem like a level of detail and rigour you weren't prepared for, but your time spent now will pay back in the confidence you'll have in the data and insights you emerge with.

Getting attitudinal

Seeking participants with certain behavioural traits is important, and straightforward to elicit, but narrowing people down by how they think about your subject matter takes a little creativity and thought on your part.

I've found a way to do this by offering sample statements about aspects of the product/service and asking the potential recruits 'Which one of these best describes how you feel about...?'

EXAMPLE:

RECRUITING FOR ATTITUDES

For the previous home-buying example, to get a feel for a person's level of support and advice required, you could ask:

Which best describes your approach to financing a home purchase?

A. I know what I can borrow so once I've found the place I want, I'll call the bank.

B. I do need a ballpark of what I can borrow, and then I can go house shopping.

C. I could do with some help to figure it so I'm looking in the right price range.

D. This is a major decision. I need all the advice and support the bank can provide.

You might then ask the recruiter to make sure they get a good mix of these, or to weight it towards home buyers with a greater need for support (C and D).

Other ways to recruit

Campaign

Advertising on a listings site such as Craigslist or via social media. While it's possible to target to specific demographics, be aware some channels can attract 'serial' participants or bias towards advocates of your product.

Online tools

Tools such as Ethnio.com allow you to sensitively and selectively target visitors to your site, inviting them to participate through a pop-up. Respondent.io places targeted ads via linkedin. These are customised services, with scheduling and participant payment built in.

'Snowball' it

Organically grow a sample by working out into the networks of just a handful of people who match the criteria, effectively making each person you find help recruit the next. This works fine if you're looking for similar people (such as nurses or students), but can be limiting if you're looking for diversity.

Direct

In many sectors, your customer or user will be so specific you'll need to lean on relationships the organisation has with its customers.

When you can get close to the action, or know someone who is (e.g., sales or customer service) work that connection, but make sure they understand what the study is about and why they're inviting customers to take part.

EXAMPLES:

TRUCK-STOP

In a project about how long-haul truckers manage their jobs, a sales connection hooked us up to camp out at a transport logistics depot in Richmond, VA. for a week, allowing us to interview truckers as they passed through in their giant rigs.

INSULIN INSIGHTS

For a project in London about using a prototype insulin pump, a clinical specialist introduced us to appropriately selected members of a diabetes support group.

10 AM JAQUIE
123 This St
2 PM CHARLES
345 The Other Ave.
Holiday
District Museum
40 mins
driv

LOGISTICS

Right people, right place, right time

That rolls off the tongue nicely, but scheduling people to take time out of their busy days on specific dates takes a lot of juggling. It's some serious administrational overhead and best left to your recruiter.

Whenever a client suggests they'd like to find their own sample from their customer base, I ask them whether they have someone who can dedicate at least a couple of days spread over a week to get this done? And who also happens to be charming ...

Geography and timing

If you're doing more than one interview or visit per day, you don't want to be flapping about getting to the next session on time. A good recruiter will account for distances and travel time, grouping your appointments in a similar area on the same day, making allowances for rush-hour traffic, etc.

How long?

A visit could be anything from an hour to a day, depending largely on participant availability and the activities you'd like to observe.

One hour is an acceptable timeframe for most people and a minimum for a useful interview, but if you need to observe someone assembling a flat-pack BBQ it would be wise to double this (and carry a spare hex key). To understand how couriers use parcel tracking systems you may need to ride shotgun for a day, or however long their round lasts. Whatever the duration, make sure the participant is clear on their commitment.

Between sessions

Try to limit visits to 2–3 per day, and make sure you allow time for your own needs.

Let your recruiter (or whoever's scheduling) know what works for you. Tell them your flight times, explain you need time between sessions to write up notes, and remind them you need a lunch and dinner break. Without this you'll be running on snacks and tracking down public toilets in stolen moments.

I'll go over icebreakers later, but, from experience, arriving at a participant's house needing to pee didn't make it on that list.

Saying thankyou

For healthcare or socially minded projects, people may offer their time in exchange for the feeling of wanting to contribute to society.

That's a feel-good factor money can't buy. For everyone else, there's Mastercard. Most research is commercially driven, and recruiting people to take part is a transaction – a value exchange.

Paying people acknowledges them for their time. It shows you value their participation in your project (and offers some security they'll actually front on the day).

Cash is king

Wherever possible and culturally appropriate, make your incentive in the form of folding cash or a loaded cash card. Most recruiting firms offer a convenient electronic bank payment to their participants, but folding cash is a universal language.

Offering product in exchange for time can influence participants and skew your findings. I remember a project where the client insisted offering either a choice of cash or a higher-dollar discount off the price of the product. After a warm response to the product, all chose the cash, sending a confusing message to the client.

If paying participants is a challenge for your organisation, try work-arounds like fuel, grocery or store vouchers, or even donations to charity.

How much?

Take recruiters' advice on setting the amount. It's a balance – you don't want to over-pay, attracting people who might not be eligible, doing it just for the money, but the rate needs to be fair and worth their while.

A student will likely fill a gap between lectures for less than a commodities trader measuring her time by the minute, or second. This usually means paying higher amounts to attract professionals, but not always.

Once when a self-employed attorney dropped his hourly charge-out rate into the conversation, it was double the 'professional' incentive he'd just been paid.

'Knowing your hourly rate, what makes it worth your while to spend an hour with me for this?' I asked. His one-word answer: 'Windfall'. His fees were spoken for, but the bunch of twenties in the back pocket were an unexpected bonus and worth more to him as a result. 'That's my Friday night taken care of', he grinned.

Paperwork

Filling out a form seems incompatible with the atmosphere you're aiming for and can be a sobering reminder of the transactional nature of a field visit, but without your participant's signature, you're stumped.

It's usually somewhere between a 'terms and conditions' and a record of the participant's involvement in the project.

I try to keep this to half a page, but depending on the nature of the project, the paperwork can become more involved.

The basics are usually:

- confirmation they understand the nature and purpose of the work
- agreement to take part
- confirmation of receipt of payment
- signature, name and details

Beyond these lie legal aspects around keeping both parties' information safe:

- NDA/Confidentiality – agreement they won't talk about the activity or materials they were exposed to
- Consent for the session to be recorded (Audio/Video/Stills) and limitations to use and storage of recordings
- Your obligations around data protection and privacy

A word on timing

Leaving the awkwardness of the paperwork to the end might suit you, but it's not in the best interests of the participant, or the project.

Over time I've realised a few reasons to get the paperwork out of the way in the first few minutes:

I see, so this is just market research?

It gives the participant assurance you, the activity and motivations are legitimate, and cements why you're with them.

How many people are you visiting?

It provides a 'threshold' moment where the participant feels they can raise questions.

Oh, but we haven't even started!

Paying the incentive upfront often surprises, but it removes any perception the payment is 'performance' related; that they'll be 'earning' their payment by saying the right things.

This won't be on YouTube, right?

You need their consent to make any of the data you collect usable.

Doh!

Leaving paperwork until the end makes it much easier to forget, leaving without their autograph.

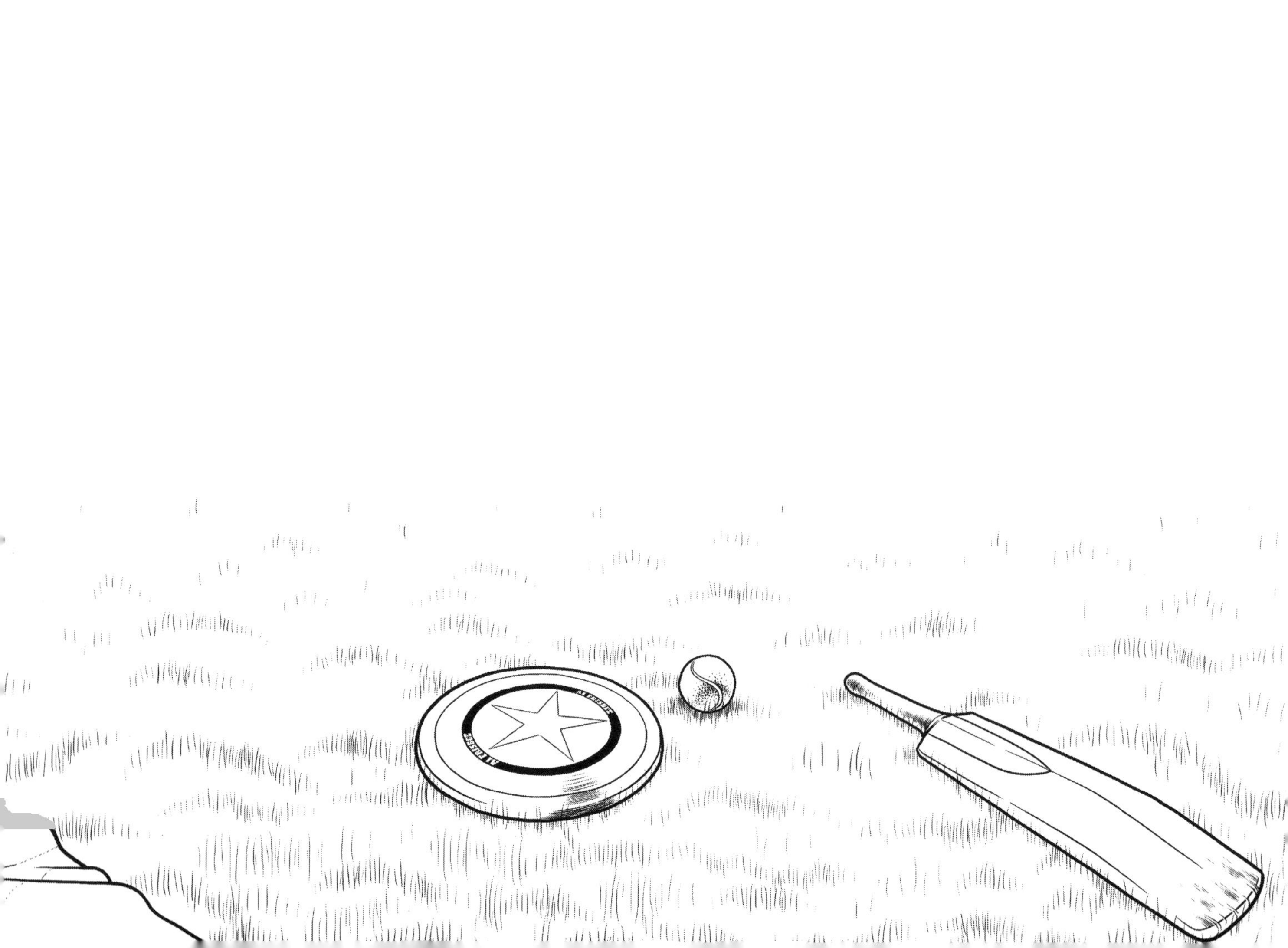

4. FIELDWORK

Context. Pre-flight. Icebreaking. Conversations. Tools for talking. Happy endings

CONTEXT

The places you'll go ...

The closer you can get to experiencing your customers' reality the deeper your understanding will be.

Fieldwork is an immersive experience: being with your customer, in context, while they interact with a product or experience.

It's more than simply place, though. Understanding a person's surroundings, lifestyle and circumstances will bring a vital layer of relevance and meaning.

Context can also be situational, emotional, cultural, social, and be dynamic from moment to moment.

Your approach to understanding this can be measured in units of physical and/or emotional proximity – how well you can connect with the people and behaviour you're trying to learn about.

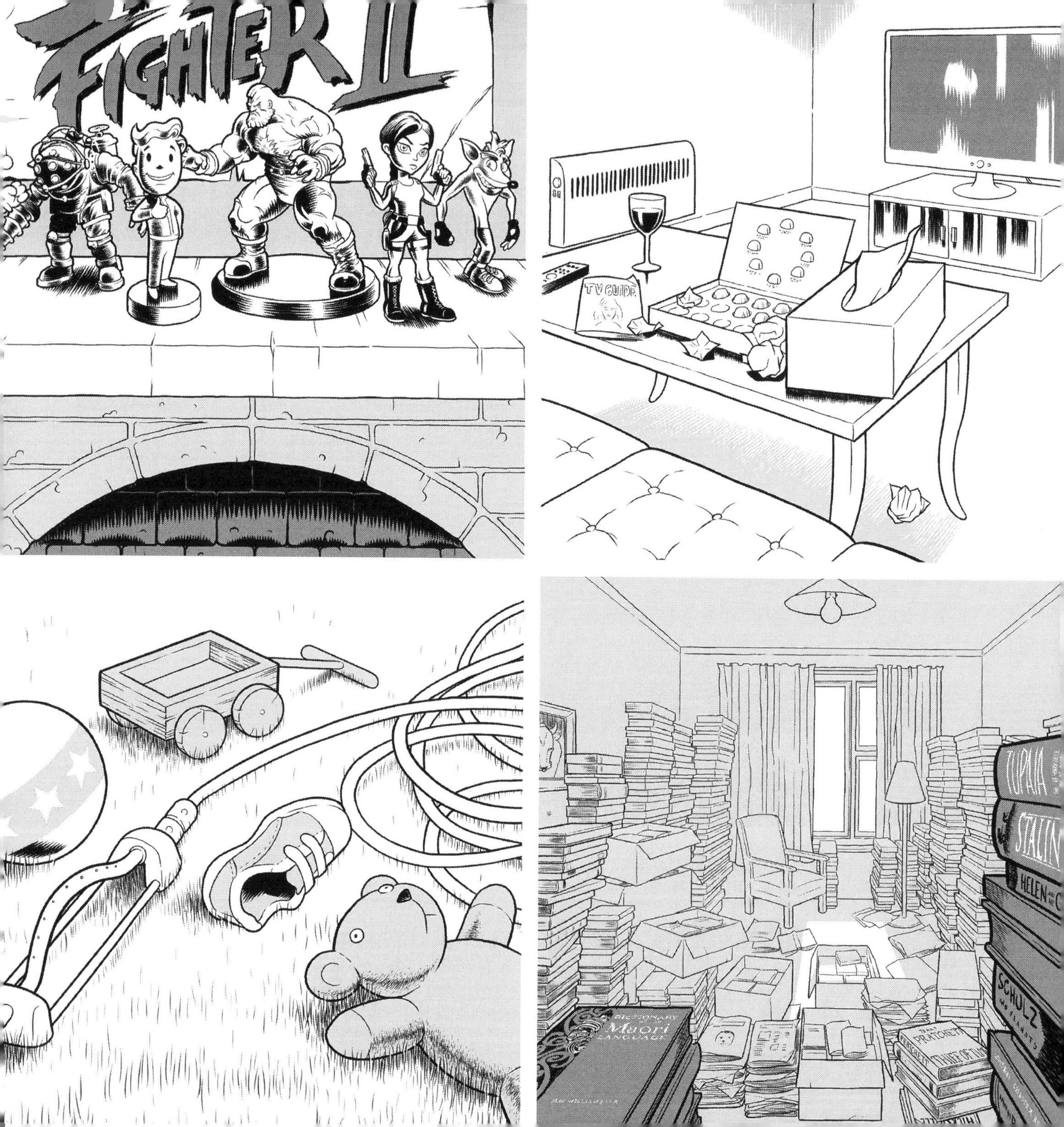
FIGHTER II
TV GUIDE
TUPAIA
STALIN
HELEN
SCHULZ
DICTIONARY
Maori
LANGUAGE
TERRY PRATCHETT
PRATCHETT
THIEF OF TI

Home sweet home

Homes speak volumes about our values.

Being with a customer where they live or work lets you see them surrounded by the props and tools, information and distractions they live with.

Their environment provides an abundance of clues as to how they think, what they value, their aspirations, interests, and what matters to them.

A half-finished DIY project, Star Wars figures in a glass case, a gardener tending their border outside or a toddler vying for their attention – all these things help complete a picture – reference points to add meaning and texture to their story.

So when considering where to conduct an interview, always take the option of a participant's home over a sterile meeting room or neutral cafe.

The value of immersion

Putting yourself directly into your customer's position opens your senses to what they're experiencing, helping you reach below the surface of what you're observing in their behaviour or what they're describing to you.

For me this has meant applying for loans, shopping for prime-cut steaks at boutique butchers (tricky territory for a vegetarian), attending real estate open homes, even getting nearly naked to experience a skin cancer monitoring service.

In practical terms, this can be more achievable in some scenarios than others. So if you're wanting to understand the experience of having a root-canal dental treatment, there's probably only so close you're prepared to go.

In many instances, though, it's a smart investment to spend time experiencing the moments, taking in the information, feeling and responding to the environment. Being a customer.

Picking your moment

Where a customer experience occurs in a specific (and accessible) public environment, for example retail or transportation, an immediate approach is to go to that place and intercept people in the moment - approaching them 'cold'.

This guerilla-style approach has value, but it's limited. You might leave with more (and better) questions than when you started, but you'll pay for the hit-and-run convenience with a lack of substance to the answers.

Your cheekiest charm-offensive can't get around the fact you've interrupted someone without their permission. There's a sense of artificiality. Their eyes dart around, they've got places to be, and this will be reflected in the quality of the conversation. You'll also realise this is a small part of a bigger picture of these people's lives - other moments and contexts that influence and contribute the decisions they make.

My approach is to firstly spend time in these environments looking for patterns in what people do, then conduct targeted and pre-arranged sessions to understand those behaviours.

EXAMPLE:

MONEY MOMENTS

We were asked to help a bank understand how business owners use ATMs to deposit cash.

Naturally, these people would not appreciate being approached in the street without warning, let alone remain in the street to discuss their routine. At best we'd have cagey, guarded responses to our enquiries.

Pre-arranging a visit to their business, followed by a trip to the ATM allowed us to gain their trust and understand the back-story to the banking task. This way their behaviour was unaffected, and made sense when we saw it played out later.

There are certainly times when being 'Johnny on the spot' will work in your favour. If you're wanting to understand what matters to mountain bikers when they're transporting their bikes, head to the carpark at the bottom of a busy trail. Same goes for luggage at an airport carpark.

For work in hospital environments, I prefer to 'cold call' on patients inviting them to share their experiences at their bedsides. This lacks the certainty of appointments but adds in-the-moment authenticity you simply don't get if people have the chance to collect their thoughts and arrange themselves in advance.

For a business-to-business product, you'll want to soak up the commercial environment your customers inhabit. Watching them go about their day, enquiring around key interactions, then perhaps retreating to a quiet, private space for an in-depth interview where you can reflect on those moments you've been part of is useful.

In a commercial setting, ensure you have permission and are introduced by and as a colleague. This allows employees to see you not as a threat, clam up or put their best foot forward. You want to hear the full story, not just the 'company line'.

Whatever the context, respect the fact you're entering another person's world, with sometimes unspoken norms, conventions, etc. These make it both easier and more difficult to do your job. They take subtlety, charm and tact to navigate, but equally provide a frame of reference. All of this would be lost if your only approach was to invite the participant to a meeting room in your office.

So pick your moment - make sure you use 'guerilla' for what it's best for: observing the 'what?' (behaviour in the moment), but try to complement this with scheduled conversations with customers to reach a deeper 'why?'

CONTEXT

EXAMPLE:

RESEARCH ON THE ROAD

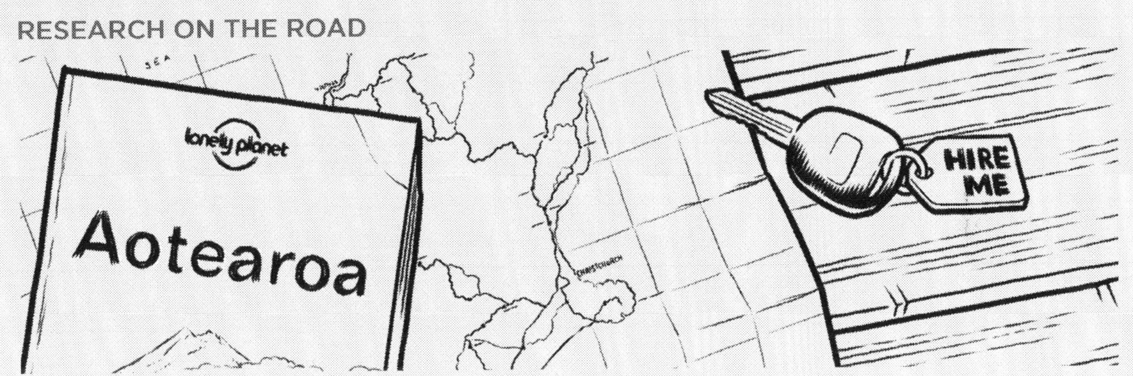

A favourite project of mine required a colleague and me to literally take a camping road trip.

Our brief, from the world's largest motorhome rental operator, was to understand the tourist experience of travelling by motorhome.

Tough gig, I hear you say. We were doing what anthropologists call 'participant observation'.

Parking up and staying alongside real tourists in motor-camps moved us across an invisible line. We felt like part of the rolling tribe. When approaching campers to hear their stories, we were seen less as nosey researchers and more as fellow travellers. This was the closest I'd been to experiencing 'instant' rapport as a researcher. Because we had an experience in common to connect over, there was little ice to break, making it easy to spark up a conversation.

By walking (well, driving) in their shoes, we were also relying on the same tools they used, like maps, guidebooks, facilities, etc. We fell into the rhythm of the campsites, observing and being part of activities happening at different times of day/evening.

It might not always mean a camping trip, but sometimes the best way to understand something is to become part of it.

CONTEXT

Far-flung and in other tongues

If your customers or end users are a visitor's visa and long-haul flight away, in an unfamiliar culture or emerging market, you owe it to the gods of context to visit them.

Video calls and online diary tools can provide a window into their lives, but immersing yourself (and your client if possible) directly into the world of the customer is something I try not to compromise on. The travel expenses will repay you ten to one in pure insight, and you'll 'feel' it, too. If seeing is believing, feeling is knowing.

Field studies in foreign territories require significantly more planning, logistics and resources, often adding a translator and maybe a guide or local researcher to your crew. A tradeoff to accept during the fieldwork stage of this type of project lies in the size of your team, which could be four or more. Intimacy is replaced with entourage, but to gain depth of insight you're going to need connection and trust, which starts with a common language.

In countries where it's not feasible to limit the sample to people who speak your language, you'll need to partner up with a bilingual local researcher and translator to work as a duo. A good translator operates in real-time, elicits meaning, picks up on humour, subtleties, cues and intonation. They're indispensable if you want to go beyond the surface.

Degrees of being there

When realities like project scope, geography, timelines, practicalities or budget conspire and you absolutely can't be there, hire a local researcher who can.

Using an in-market research partner shouldn't mean outsourcing, or an all-or-nothing arrangement. There are many stages of involvement worth considering:

- joining the initial days of fieldwork provides a valuable chance to work with the researcher, refining the direction and boundaries of your study.
- being part of the analysis or synthesis will allow you to maximise the relevance of the findings to your business needs.
- flying them out at the tail end to share their insights can bring the voice of the customer into the room, adding texture and cultural meaning you might only be able to hint at.

PRE-FLIGHT

Roles and responsibilities

The perfect team size in the field is two - a lead and a supporting role.

Given you're reading this book, you're likely the lead, and it may be your client or a team member joining you for the fieldwork. Whether you're with an experienced colleague or a newbie client, it's important you know which role you are playing before you knock on a participant's door.

With a few visits under your belt you will develop a 'double act', knowing how each other behaves. You'll know when the other is in the flow or when to step in. You're a team.

(It is possible to do this solo, too, and with all the responsibility on yourself, there are no arguments over who does what.)

LEAD

Meet and greet the participant, break the ice, explain the project, then bring your curiosity to the conversation.

Introduce your partner: a subtle but important task and one which should be discussed prior to arrival. I usually err towards downplaying their role as I introduce them, whether they're a seasoned researcher or a client riding shotgun for the first time.

'This is Nicole, my trusty note-taker. She'll be mostly listening, but might have a few questions at the end because I usually miss things.'

An experienced side-kick will be in tune with this but it's important a client/team-member knows what to expect in terms of their 'status' in the room.

Remember: the participant needs to trust and feel comfortable with who's in the room, so use discretion and be fully transparent about roles when required.

SUPPORT

Beyond taking notes, this role takes the heat off the lead so they can focus on their connection with the participant.

Document the session – take notes, handle video/audio recording and photography.

While mostly 'blending in', be super observant, following the cadence and rhythm of the conversation and remaining very present.

Occasionally the interviewer will seem to 'drown' in the conversation, reaching a point of interview inertia – a bit like writer's block. This is your 'Baywatch moment': dive in, rescue, and maintain the flow by interjecting or looping in with a clarifying question. Staying in-tune with the conversation will help you see these moments coming, or recognise when the lead is deliberately using an uncomfortably long pause to allow the participant to open up, without wanting a prompt.

'Housekeeping' items the lead will love you for taking care of include: schedule/timing, paperwork, consent forms, incentives, organising prototype stuff or props for activities ...

... plus finding the best places to debrief and refuel.

Lose the script

In my earliest projects at a UX research agency I'd work directly from a script that had been signed off by the client. Sometimes it was called a 'protocol'. It was all too rigid for me. I'd recite this list of prompts to each participant like I was a robot, sometimes taking liberties by switching up the order of questions.

I'd been told I should ask the same questions to all participants to maintain consistency, but it felt awkward working to a script and as if I were hearing only half of the story.

Over time, my approach evolved to something more conversational, as a way to pry into that other half of the story not being told.

This may sound like a convenient way to take the effort and rigour out of the process, but it doesn't make it any easier. Instead, you need to run a mental cache of everything the participant says and does, noting where the conversation has been, and making on-the-fly decisions about where it's headed:

Should I probe further on that comment or let it slide?

Did she just contradict herself?

Should I ask her to show me the app on her phone now, or get her to explain it first?

How much time do we have left?

... and all the while you're trying to make the participant feel like the conversation is following natural twists and turns, rather than being simultaneously monitored and steered by you, the interviewer.

Conversational territories

Generally, I will first agree on a set of objectives with the team. This describes the territory we'd like to cover during the conversation and reads like a list of topics around which we'd like to learn. Some of these might be framed as questions when you verbalise them, but it's far from being a script. It is a set of questions to which I feel the need to answer in my own head, before I begin planning the interviews.

You need to feel your client or team's blind-spots and the weight of the decisions on the table. This requires an understanding of the business, product and design context and should be embedded in your curiosity. The flow of the conversation and your choice of questions with a participant should come naturally if you've built up this level of understanding of your client's position.

Piloting your conversation with someone suitable before you hit the road will give you a feel for how much ground you can cover, types of questions which work (and don't) and the flow between topics.

Going cold turkey

A researcher's most valuable trait is a vulnerable one. When heading out to a field visit, I find having too much prior knowledge about that person can dull my curiosity and influence my thoughts with facts I'm better off without.

Here's an example of how I try to maintain my curiosity:
The recruiter provides a schedule and participant list with granular details of every participant. Along with name, address and contacts will be their demographics, customer type, attitudes and attributes, collected when they were screened. To maintain my curiosity, I pick only three of these details to stick to the car dashboard: time of appointment, first name, address.

I do this for two reasons. Firstly, I want to be an empty vessel; not knowing makes me hungry to discover. That's fuel in my curiosity tank. Secondly, I want to interview a person, not a 'customer segment'. I don't want any judgements to creep in as to whom I'm about to meet, or to influence my line of questioning.

Going in cold takes some getting used to. It's part of trusting your instinct and being comfortable with ambiguity – both things you'll need later in analysis. So, consider this a warm-up exercise.

EXAMPLE:

WHEN LESS IS MORE

On a project for a client with a subscription-based product, we interview a mix of subscribers, non-subscribers and ex-subscribers. All three are relevant.

Without knowing who sits in each category, we therefore can't pigeon-hole them in our minds before we walk in the door. We don't want them to feel like they've been 'picked for a reason', or for them to play a certain role/character.

If we know 'A' is an ex-customer, we could be wondering, 'why did she cancel her subscription?', looking for clues, reading between the lines, or this may draw to the surface before she's had a chance to fully describe her context. Or she might detect this thread and defend her reasons for leaving the service, which isn't what we want to hear.

It is better to let these details come out, in the customers' words, from a natural, unbiased conversation in response to sincere enquiry, rather than feigned naivety.

In this way, when a participant mentions why they're tempted to drop the service for the competitor, we can genuinely ask which service they're with.

Tip Top
KIA ORA DAIRY
Tip Top
Tip Top
HOT PIES
Tip Top
KIA ORA DAIRY
Tip Top
Tip Top
HOT PIES
216

ICEBREAKING

Neighbourhood icebreakers

Building a picture of a person begins in the street. Their street. Clues about lifestyle, living arrangements, values and beliefs are all there in their immediate neighbourhood.

I always aim to arrive early, eyeball the participant's address, then switch into a mindset as if I were looking to move into the area. I'll take a drive around a few neighbouring streets, take a short walk in a local park, have a cuppa from a local cafe, or buy something from the corner store.

You may need to improvise in industrial or rural areas, but building a little familiarity like this provides a contextual anchor and a layer of local knowledge that can become common ground for an icebreaker conversation.

'That's a handy corner shop you've got there – looks like they have one of just about everything!'

As well as being invitations masquerading as observations, I use them to connect with the participant. They might respond with their own thoughts or experiences – and reveal something about themselves:

'Yeah, he sells one of everything ...
... except a good coffee ...

... and the conversation rolls on as you're taking off your shoes.

Soaking your senses

My radar ramps up as I approach the house, like a detective, looking for signs about their lifestyle.

A boat or 'project' car in the driveway is a dead cert for a revealing chat you could extend for an hour, but be ready to settle for a cactus collection on the windowsill.

With brief introductions out of the way and shoes kicked off, I'll launch straight into:

'So, I'm picking you're the cactus whisperer of the house?'

If you can pitch the level of chat around a familiar topic, it takes the edge off the weirdness of the situation, and makes it easier for them to begin to open up.

Soaking up visual cues in these first minutes of entering a home lets you build an inventory of fodder for small talk but also a possible 'hook' related to the project at hand. If it's a travel-related project, holiday snaps, souvenirs or travel guides on the bookshelf will pop. If the project is about food, I'll spot the barbeque on the terrace, the kombucha fermenting on the bench.

Remember, personal and relatable topics around the participant reinforces the focus and tone of the visit – that it's all about them.

ICEBREAKING

Finding the comfort zone

A participant will either take you straight to a place where they are comfortable or ask you:

So, where do you want to do this?

Even if the project is about lawn-mowing and you'll need to spend time in the yard or shed, try to feel out where the hub of the home is.

Given the option, I'll always gravitate towards the kitchen table. It's often surrounded by the props and evidence of daily life: a pile of bills, a chicken thawing, a tired vase of flowers. The person is in their zone, but it means there's also a table to spread any activities out.

In a workplace there's much less personality on show, so you'll need to work harder to find something to connect over, perhaps props that reveal something about their personality or professional approach.

In a corporate environment, you'll want to take the participant's lead on where comfortable is for them. The staff kitchen might not be a place they're happy to share more than a bowl of snacks in.

Take a seat
I try not to sit opposite the participant. It's less confrontational at an angle, and easier to adjust personal space for the right level of intimacy.

Or not ...
When it comes to seating, it's about the participant being comfortable, even if you're not. If there aren't enough seats (and even sometimes when there are), you could park yourself on the floor. I do this by default in situations where I want to avoid power imbalance.

Sure, the floor might mean cat hair, damp and probably cramp, but being at a lower level gives the participant the 'status' in the room; it sets up a dynamic that says 'I'm here to listen'. The right dynamic is worth more than your own comfort.

Grace and charm

Together, they sound like a sit-com, but this duo will go a long way in helping to un-weird the situation for you and the participant.

Be the perfect house guest.
Take off your shoes, thank the participant at least once at the beginning of the visit, make them know their time is appreciated. *'Oh, thanks so much for taking time out of your day for us.'*

Respect their time.
In most situations, research participants have you time-boxed. Remind them of the time you'll be done near the start. This shows you value their time and allows them to relax about future arrangements they might have. Also, stick to your finishing time.

If they offer, accept.
I nearly fainted with delight when in one home visit I was greeted with: *'You must be tired from talking to people all day, I've put on a batch of shortbread.'* And then later leaving with a few 'roadies' in a zip-loc bag. This is what made this participant comfortable. I was her guest and shortbread was her way of being relaxed with a stranger in her home.

I've had the same happen with deer penis and caterpillar fungus broth and had to take it in my stride. So, whether it's a drink, somewhere to hang your coat or the offer to bring your car into the driveway off the busy highway, accept graciously.

Be complimentary.
Behave like you'd want to be invited back, even though you know this might never happen.

ICEBREAKING

Rapport

Interviews are built on this magical stuff – it's a quality of connection you make with the person; a level of social comfort underpinned by trust.

If you were on a date you'd call it 'chemistry', and in a field visit there's a discernible moment you know you've unlocked it. A mutual laugh at a sarcastic comment will do nicely, maybe a knowing pause is all you need to make the transition.

Becoming comfortable with a stranger in their home within a few minutes will test anyone's social skills, but time spent establishing rapport is a good investment for the quality of an interview.

Finding a spark

This connection can spark on many levels: energy, humour, a shared interest or a mutual viewpoint. But the best way I've found is via an engaged and responsive dialogue.

If you haven't found something from your scope of the neighbourhood to use as a conversation starter (and there's no wall-sized tropical fish tank to 'wow' at), offer a personalised version of *'I love what you've done with the place'*, commenting on an aspect of their space, location, outlook, and so on.

These familiar topics are easy ground to cover. Before you know it they've mentioned kids or pets, recent or upcoming changes in their life, or they're apologising for the 'state of the place' because of the renovation work in progress. Any of these doors are worth opening to find a connection.

Get specific

I've found it's possible to short-circuit the small talk by jumping straight to a specific detail. Zooming right in, then zooming out from there. Pick a physical detail – something to quickly take the focus away from the 'artificial conviviality' – with which to engage them.

I'll say:
'Now that's a snowglobe collection. Which was the first one you got?' An impossible-to-refuse invitation to talk me through the story of their collection, revealing more and more layers and threads to connect on.

Safety through vulnerability

While your grace and charm are flowing and rapport's reaching the boil, you're creating an atmosphere where it feels safe to open up and share. To find common ground is a good start, as is the chance to reveal something of your own character – I'll often be self-deprecating about a personal tendency or a weakness (there are plenty to choose from). By doing this, you're setting the bar – for what's safe to share about – by being unfiltered yourself.

Almost there

You need to dial in to the person's mood, energy and demeanour, then meet them on their level. You read it in their body language.

This can be subtle, but if the participant's arms are crossed and their knee is jiggling like a teenager on their first date, you've got some work to do. So, don't start the interview until that knee is still or you've somehow managed to 'crack the nut'.

Stay off-topic

Although out of nerves they might try to, you don't want them to get started from the get-go talking about the topic, product or behaviour you're there to learn about. If this happens, politely but firmly acknowledge their enthusiasm and deflect:

'Oh, that's great, it sounds like you have some experience with the healthcare system. In a few minutes we'd love to learn your story, but first ... those snowglobes!'.

ICEBREAKING

Getting down to business

When it comes to introducing the project and objectives, I use a sliding scale of disclosure.

Some people just want to get on with the conversation; others need the full back-story before they feel relaxed enough to dive in. Therefore, in the first few minutes of meeting a person, I'm making a judgement on where they sit on this scale and how I'll play it.

Rather than being totally business-like: *'Okay, so today I'm here to ...'*, I open with something like: *'So, what were your thoughts when you were asked to take part in this?'*

Their response helps me check what they've been told during recruitment and any preconceptions they might have. Hearing it in their terms stops me introducing any business-speak and whether they want to know more or are happy to roll from there.

If it's clear they are across why we're here and what to expect, I'll simply confirm their summary. *'Well, that's better than I could have said it.'*

Other times I'll detect the participant would like some gaps filled: *'Why was I picked?'; 'Where are you from again?'; 'How will this information be used?'*

In these cases, I'll paint a fuller picture, but still with a broad brush.

Something like:
'The people planning what they want to do next at (client or anonymous) feel a bit in the dark as to what people really think about this stuff and what the experience is like, so they figure by talking with a range of people they might get a better idea of what it's like to be you, and to see things from your point of view.'

I don't want to dwell on or overcook the intro, leading them to overthink it. As I'm explaining this, I watch for subtle non-verbal cues. They let me know whether this is hitting the spot or not. If they're biting their lip, I'll ask: *'Is there something you're not quite sure about?'* I make sure I explain until they're satisfied.

Be open. Be transparent.
If there's an ounce of uncertainty or the participant doesn't trust you, you're wasting your and their time.

Is it a privacy thing? Are they concerned about what you'll do with the footage? You have to figure out what they need to know to be comfortable; then defuse it, and move into the good stuff.

CONVERSATIONS

Talking to learn

Talking is a social and survival skill you've likely mastered. A good thing, because along with observation, interviewing is going to be a staple in your design-research diet. You'd starve without it.

But interviewing isn't talking as you're used to. It's a deliberate learning exercise, loaded with techniques you'll need to re-learn ... because you used to be better at it.

As kids we relied on asking questions to understand our world. As we headed through school we were taught knowledge and answers hold more value, so we stopped asking questions and sought answers instead.

Interviewing, as a research approach, is conversation driven by curiosity, loaded with seat-of-the-pants techniques and changing on the fly. When you're doing it well, it's absolutely exhausting.

Minimum requirements

Being a good listener and empathetic might be handy baseline traits, but interviewing is a mind and skillset honed over time.

I'm self-taught, cutting my teeth during usability tests for websites, but my mindset was always: 'How can I learn the most in the precious 60 minutes I have with this stranger?'

I was a few dozen interviews in when I started really paying attention to technique, consciously employing tactics during a conversation, noticing how the little things, such as a pause or repeating a single word, can change the course of a conversation.

A few dozen more and I realised that success doesn't come down to mastery of technique. It depends on how much you care.

An embedded curiosity, combined with basic social skills (be nice, listen, eye contact) and a deep desire to learn, will go further than all the technique in the world compared to someone who's only half interested.

It's personal, instinctive, and highly situational. Some people play loose, others are more methodical. You'll need to develop your own style as you discover what works for you.

Meet the other expert

You'll need an open, naïve mindset - even if this makes you appear to know far less than you do about the product or market.

At the end of 20 interviews I'll still say, *'Sorry, what did you call that thing again?'* nodding quizzically at a technical term I've been hearing all week.

This 'feigning naivety' might seem (ok it is) disingenuous, but the last thing I want is for a participant to edit or filter their choice of words because they assume I know what they're talking about.

You might be a product expert, but the participant is an expert in their experience with your product.

We're the students, not the teacher, so keep your knowledge under your hat.

Knowledge can inadvertently slip out during an interview when you:

- introduce yourself as the global Head of Digital Strategy
- say *'Really?!'* when they mention how they do something
- introduce an industry term or phrase (unless they've used it themselves)
- correct a word they're saying incorrectly
- finish their sentence in a knowing way
- nod approvingly or exclaim 'Awesome!' at their description of something they do or think
- scribble furiously at your notes like you're reeling in a 40-kilogram tuna
- tell them how you usually do it
- offer 'insider' industry advice

So, as you turn up to each interview, leave all the product, technical, brand or marketing knowledge (which makes you great at your work) behind. It will still be there when you get back, but with a little customer knowledge to boot.

The anatomy of an interview

Every conversation has its own pace, rhythm, balance, energy.
Some are more meandering, others are like a series of chapters.
If there was such a thing as an 'average' interview, it might look like this:

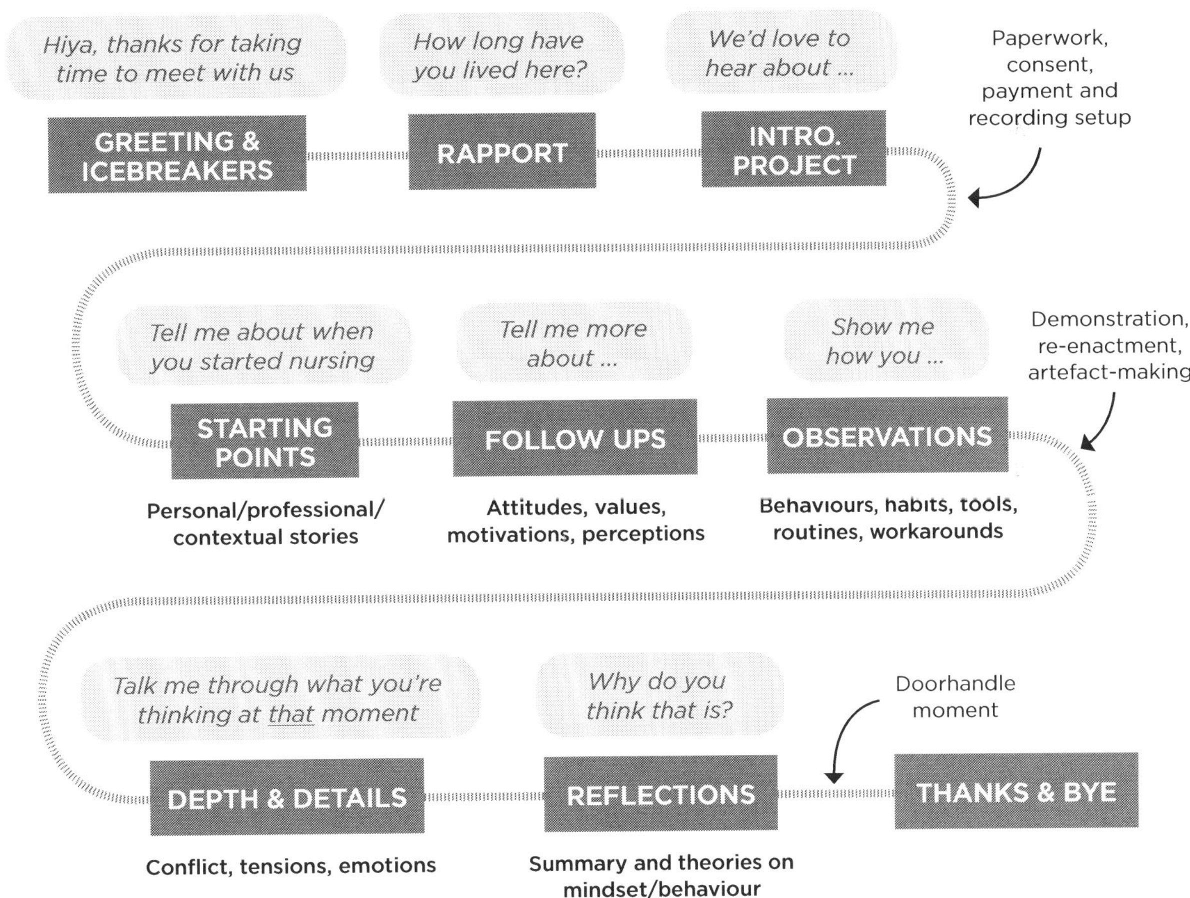

CONVERSATIONS

Reaching story point

As a kid, you never asked for a 'bedtime fact'. You wanted a story, with a central character, in an unfolding world of intriguing experiences; something with context, narrative and tension.

Start at the beginning
Asking a person to recollect a point in time can provide a great springboard. When interviewing a patient about their experience in a hospital bed, I've started with: *'So, where did this all begin for you?'* When the project was about buying motorhomes and I was sitting in one, with its owners: *'Take me back to the moment you knew buying a motorhome was on the cards'*

Watch their eyes roll back and to the left as the interview jumps into life, giving you a window into theirs.

Consider it your goal – early in an interview – to bring a story to the surface.

A typical pattern for getting to this point is to follow a question/answer/question/answer dialogue ... until an answer contains a hook you can fish up a story with.

Maybe it's a moment you'd like the participant to bring to life. It can be as simple as the word 'sometimes' or 'eventually', alluding to a moment passed. This is your ticket. Lean in, then repeat the word (with the rising tone of a question mark on the end).

Be attentive, encouraging them to flesh out the details of their account of a specific interaction or chain of events as they experienced it.

Within the factual narrative lies expressions of their worldview and values, perceptions and emotions for you to uncover ... by asking more questions.

Reaching 'story point' early makes it clear to the participant this is not a survey – you're giving them permission to go deep about what's unique to them: it's their story, and the details matter. Do this well and you'll set up for a great interview, with perhaps several *'Oh, and this one time ...'* extra stories.

Of course there will be times when you have to use your utmost diplomacy to keep a participant on track – and sometimes you need to head them off at the pass before everything becomes a story.

Airtime

You're at a cafe catching up with a friend.

Unless one of you has had a major life event, you'll probably split the air-time around 50:50. You, as much as they, have things to say, so you're jockeying for your 50 per cent, looking for an entry. You'll take turns.

An interview, however, has a different ratio. You'd be wanting to split the air-time around 90:10 – with them having the 90 per cent. Which means you need to use your 10 per cent very wisely.

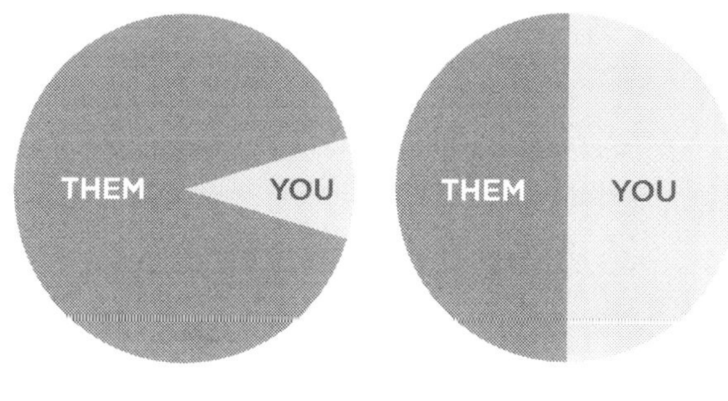

Aim for this

Not this

Think how a talk-show host sets up their guests, using a primer such as, *'What was it like putting on all that weight for the role in the film?'*

We soak up anecdotes between the host's short prompts, but learn little about the host because the host knows their audience is interested in the guests, not the host.

Louis Theroux, a legendary TV journalist, has a more conversational interviewing style. In terms of air-time, the split might be closer to 75:25.

Louis has perfected the art of taking the audience into controversial, sensitive subjects, seemingly getting the answers without always asking the question. He's a master at building rapport, disarming his subjects, then putting them on the spot with direct questions in a non-threatening way.

Watch five minutes of any of his interviews and you'll pick up 20 techniques.

Golden rules

A few solid Do's and 'Don'ts exist around how you frame your questions and how you choose your words (or not).

All the following rules are geared around promoting openness and keeping you from introducing bias:

THE DON'TS:

No leading

Don't suggest the answer you're looking for in the question.
'How well does this integrate with your workflow?' is what the product manager wants to know, but the participant will detect this and it might influence their response; they then tell you what they think you want to hear.

No selling

Don't introduce any subjective language when referring to a product or service: *'Now compare how efficient this is to our more streamlined version'*. This positions you as invested in a specific solution and tells the participant what you believe about the product. Who are they to disagree?

No future talk

People's predictions of what they'll do tomorrow are unreliable at best, so stick with the present and the things they've actually done. A good rule of thumb is to stop yourself from beginning questions with *'if ...'*

Let's roll these three naughties into one burrito of bad enquiry:

So, ***how useful*** *would it be* ***if there was*** *a* ***simple new tool*** *to* ***help you do that a different, better way?***

- **how useful** … **Leading**
- **if there was** … **Future talk**
- **simple new tool** … **Selling**
- **help you do that a different, better way?** … **Leading, Selling & Future talk**

THE DO'S:

Break the rules

There are no penalties for breaking these rules, but it would be a crime to accept the answer to this 'loaded' question on face value.
By following up with targeted queries:

'Why exactly would that be useful?'; 'What if there weren't such a tool?'; 'Wouldn't simple take away from that detail you love?' etc, and we're suddenly a couple of layers deeper.

I'm not suggesting a 'bait, then interrogate' approach, but be aware of conversational roads you close (and open) when you pose a loaded question like this.

Be neutral

We know not to express disappointment or approval at things participants say or do. We don't show surprise with *'really?'* or give a pat on the back with *'Awesome'* when an *'uh huh'* will do.

But again ... there are times to break these rules.

Do ask *'really?'* if the participant appears to be contradicting themselves, referring to what they said or did earlier.

Do egg them on to show you more if someone's proudly showing how they 'hacked' a product in their workshop to make it work better for them. There's no room for a dead-pan *'uh-huh'* there.

Speak native

Do use words such as stuff, whatsit, doo-da to refer to things at the start of an interview until they've introduced all the technical words and brand names themselves.

We can learn a lot from the words people use to describe things and the things they do. By introducing our own industry jargon, we lose that opportunity.

Shut up

Do embrace silence. Make space for the person to talk, or to think, then talk.

Make sure you walk away with those things they nearly didn't say. All it takes is five seconds.

Just when you feel there's an uncomfortably long pause, make a conscious effort not to fill the void. Seconds can seem like minutes, but often you'll be rewarded by a participant reframing or adding useful, deeper layers to their story.

Acknowledge

Early in a conversation their willingness to fill a silence may represent nerves, but later, the trust you've built will be rewarded as they take the opportunity to share things, which may come from well below the surface.

Do respect that the person is giving of themselves possibly more than they bargained for when agreeing to be part of your study. At an appropriate moment, thank them for their candour.

ARTFORUM

Ask a better question

An interview is a conversation with a purpose.

Questions fuel and steer the dialogue to deliver on this purpose.

So it pays to look at the questions you're asking and how you're asking them.

There are many ways to invite and encourage dialogue - to peel back layers of meaning - to get to those answers.

In between your direct staple 'W' questions - What, Who, When Why & hoW - will be dozens of things you'll say, but can't plan for.

You'll build a repertoire of favourites and know which one to pull out when you feel like there's 'one more layer' to peel.

There are three main types of question I use:

1. STARTING POINTS
2. PROMPTS
3. QUALIFIERS

And I'll explain how these form the backbone of my technique.

CONVERSATIONS

1. Starting points:

An invitation to share or revisit a moment; triggers for a story or demonstration

'Take me back to the moment you–';
'Tell me about the last time you did that–';
'Talk me through your train of thoughts at that time–';
'Show me how you do–';

These starters lock in on a specific time and detail and are a useful way to keep people from describing simply an idealised experience.

The best time of course is 'right now'. I like to use these during the activity, as the experience itself can be a great trigger for 'stand out' moments from their back-catalogue, i.e., *'Tell me about a time things didn't go as smoothly as this.'*

Let them feel like they have all the air-time they need. Use attentive body language (lean in, eye contact, etc) to encourage them to reach that golden 'story point'.

2. Prompts:

Digging deeper when you think there's more to learn from what they say, what they do or what they say they do.

'Tell me more about that?'
'Confusing ...?'

This is where you echo an adjective they've just used, but as an open query.
'You do that most of the time?'

Repeat a few of their words and leave them to elaborate. *'So ...?'* (accompanied with a tilt of the head and mild 'throw me a bone' face) *'And in that moment you're feeling ...?'* (leaving them to lay their emotions bare).

Tune your radar to the things they say and the way they say them. When you dig like this people can seem surprised at how interested you are in a granular detail to which they haven't given much thought. Un-surprise them with genuine enquiry, but use your judgement to pick your moments.

Prompting maintains momentum, making for engaging dialogue, but when they're on a roll in the wrong direction, you'll need to hold out for a natural pause before you politely jump in to course-correct.

3. Qualifiers:

When you're wanting to make sure you understand, you think there's something a couple of layers deeper, or your bullshit detector is glowing amber.

Getting your tone just right on these is super-important. You don't want to appear like you're trying to catch them out or cross-examine.

Summary replay:
Sometimes you just want them to string together a fragmented set of thoughts scattered over the last few minutes: *'So* [offer your generalised summary with emphasis on the bits you're unsure of] *... have I got this right?'*

So which one was it?
Other times you think they've contradicted themselves and you want to know which way they really swing: *'So, you'd recommend it, but only to people who ...'* (leaving them to finish and explain why).

'Earlier you said it was too personal to talk about medical stuff with friends, but you found out about skin cancer from someone at work. So...' (leaving them to elaborate).

BS detector:
Sometimes you sense they're trying to tell you what they think you want to hear, or they're painting a rosier picture than their reality.

Play devil's advocate by offering the participant an easy 'out' for something you're not sure they're fully behind. *'Would you – like, really? That's a lot of effort ...'*

In their words:
If the conversation is becoming a bit removed from the participant's day-to-day – perhaps they've over-thought things – asking them to say it how they would to a friend can help bring back their voice.

'It sounds like you'd do a few things differently next time. Think of a friend who might be in a similar position. Let's imagine she's on the phone considering her options ... What advice do you give?'

Don't be scared of a bit of role play here. It sounds cheesy, but passing a phone or prop as if it were ringing seems to add some reality, and playing the role of the friend by coming back with a question can elicit much more.

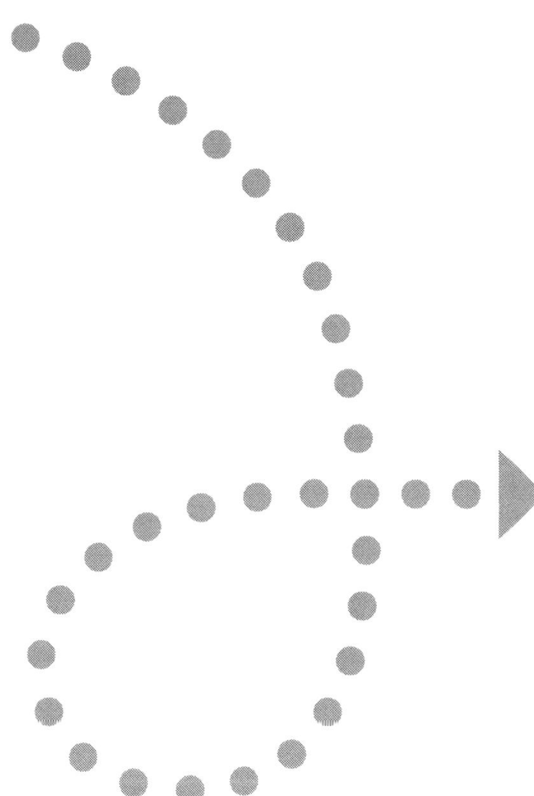

A question for yourself

Sometimes you'll draw a blank.

Saturation point.

Mental overload.

Distraction.

It happens.

When the conversation is hitting a dead end, but you feel there's more to learn from the participant, direct a silent question at yourself:

Why are we here?

Think of the design team: their challenge, the decisions they need to make to move forward. What are the assumptions? The unknowns? What would give the team confidence and what would rattle them?

Reconnecting with your purpose can be a useful, focusing nudge to reboot your curiosity and fuel some targeted questions again.

CONVERSATIONS

Mind the gap

You've got your eyes and ears on, the dialogue is flowing, you're absorbing what the person is saying, doing, thinking and feeling ...

but, sometimes what you're seeing and hearing doesn't match up.

She describes how useful a feature is - but she's only used it once.

He says it's a false economy to buy cheap - but goes straight to the sale section.

These gaps between conversation and observation may reveal tensions between their values, perceptions, intentions and actions.

They're not trying to trick you or pull the wool over your eyes. It may be they're telling us what they think we want to hear, or describing an idealised version of the truth. Perhaps.

EXAMPLE:

WHITE KNUCKLE NONCHALANCE

An example of this occurred in a banking project about ATM use.

In conversation, a taxi driver confidently described how relaxed he was when depositing the week's takings of cash in the ATM. He suggested there was not a whiff of concern about security, despite holding onto a wad of dosh.

Walking a few paces behind him to the machine we noticed his fists clench and a purposeful tap of the front pocket - full of cash - as he glanced over both shoulders, scanning the vicinity while feigning nonchalance. He was clearly on edge.

This telling tension between his desired and actual reality spoke volumes and was a critical learning moment to a team trying to improve an ATM lobby experience.

Where you find conflict like this, there will be insights. Sometimes right on the surface, other times you'll need to be diplomatic in order to help the person paint you the full picture.

Rather than being like a lawyer accusing them of a flaw in their story, play your most polite devil's advocate. Gently lay out the two sides of the story like a fascinating puzzle, inviting them to help you solve it.

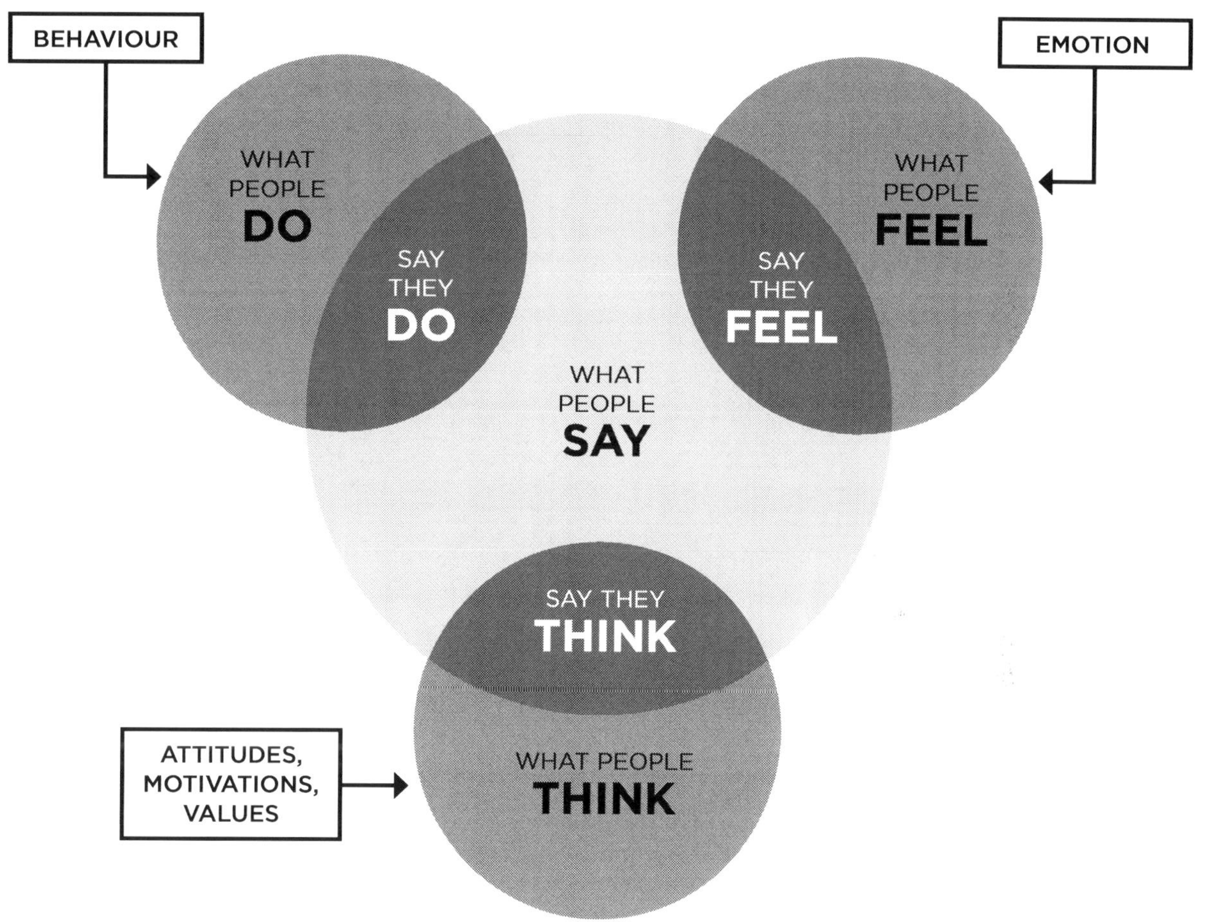

Clues around what people need lie in the overlaps and contradictions between their actions and words.

TOOLS FOR TALKING

Making the conversation visual and interactive through tangible props allows participants to build, then see 'the whole picture', so you can too.

Games people play

Game-like activities can sound tacky or juvenile (and clients may take some convincing these are more than 'child's play'), but giving customers something to arrange and/or respond to can help express perceptions, beliefs, attitudes, emotions and preferences – revealing tensions and much more.

Perhaps some people are more comfortable with something to do, or maybe they just need the visual trigger to begin a conversation. Either way, I've seen participants visibly relax and open up, letting me into their stream of thoughts, where I want to be.

Most commonly I use a variation of one of the following five:

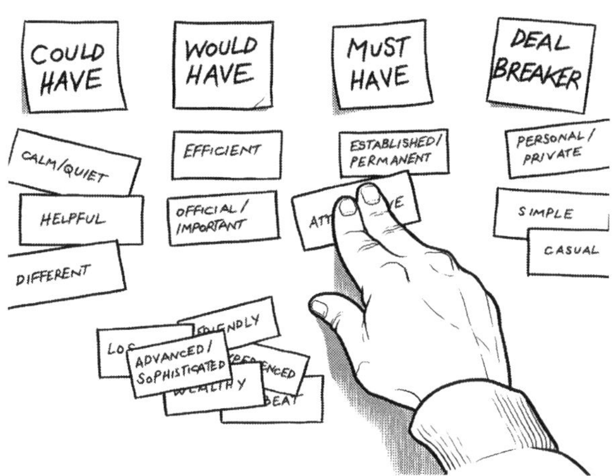

Grouping

Asking people to sort items printed on cards can reveal how they think. You can ask them to arrange and group cards into their own or pre-defined categories, by value, importance, usefulness, etc.

If, for example, you're asking people to 'rank' or 'yay/nay' aspects of a product or service by perceived utlility, always include a neutral 'maybe', 'sometimes' or 'it depends' category.

Items placed in this category are your 'swing states' where you can prompt the participant to find out what that item or function would need to offer to be moved from neutral to a definite yay or nay.

Example product feature, 'Sharing with friends?' *'Hmm ... I'd put that in maybe, because I'd need to know I could choose who could see it.'*

Journey

Plotting a sequence of events, by placing items in the order they happened, a journey map, can help a participant visualise experiences or interactions which occur over time, anything from minutes to months.

These work especially well for decision-making paths and relationships with services or environments - digital, physical or a mix of both.

They also work well in an interview immediately following an observed activity - reliving the experience in a visual format - like during a 'shop-along' study, when retail clothes' shoppers were asked to map out the stages of a retail experience. Mapping the high and low points, from entering the store, through to the fitting rooms and checkout.

TOOLS FOR TALKING

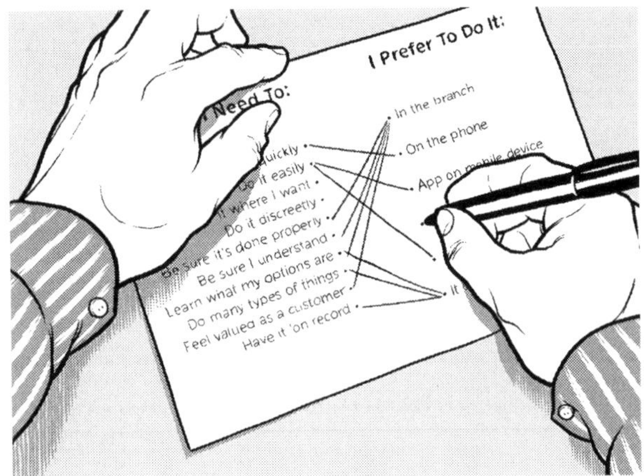

Mapping

A game of 'this goes with that'.
Asking people to join the dots between lists of items or descriptions of product functions, attributes etc. can be great for understanding why people make certain choices, associations, connections or how they perceive or feel things.

Patterns become easy to spot in the shape of the webs people draw between the lists.
For example, when I had a list of transaction types and banking channels, to understand what influences a person's decision to use one or another.

Or mapping types of TV/video content to different viewing contexts - whether people were usually viewing solo, socially, both or ...it depends. That last one is always the most interesting category to explore further.

Visual metaphor

Using an abstract and unrelated set of images can dive-bomb people's thoughts several layers deeper. It's especially useful when talking about sensitive topics.

There is no standard set out there, just pick a dozen or so images which could be interpreted in different ways and aren't necessarily related to the category. Prepare to be surprised by associations people make with the off-topic images you threw in to mix it up.

Example: Which one of these images best sums up how you feel about this? Three people could choose the picture of the duck and give you three answers to explore further: *'Because these things are like water off a duck's back to me'*, *'Because I'm kicking like mad under the water even though I'm calm on top'* or *'Because I feel guilty I've ducked out of my responsibility'*

Similarly, a ladder might represent success/ progression, or a way to escape.

Talking hands

Let your customer build their own model of a product or service and you'll soon learn what's important to them.

Their explanation about what they build can express how they think, what they believe and what their version of 'better' might look like.

This could be two dimensional – asking them to draw their ideal landing page for a website, or something more tangible, for example, using a modest set of LEGO to build a model of what they're thinking.

Perhaps hand them a lump of clay and ask them to shape it into their ideal travel mouse, as I did once for a project.

Rules of the game

Dialogue, not data

These activities are primarily about the conversation, not collecting data. While there may be some telling patterns in the arrangements, it is the thoughts they help elicit from the customer which can be most useful.

You can photograph the final arrangement, but the real value lies in what the customer has shared in describing it, justifying their selections or placements and what this means to them.

Wildcards

Consider injecting some nutty, contrary or potentially polarising items amongst the 'usual suspects'. Response to these wildcards can be more revealing than the predictable set of known items.

Freestyle

Always include a few 'blank' cards and have a pen handy. You're unlikely to have covered every eventuality or option in your set of cards or content, so let customers make their own, or make them up on the spot with them. Running the activity on a sheet of paper means customers can draw circles around groups, links between items, and so on.

Be a 'thought sniper'

In these activities, each move a person makes holds a thought we could learn from. While some will offer a running commentary, others may suit being left alone with their thoughts.

With the latter, watch their movements and mannerisms, when they bite their lip, hesitate, or second-guess themselves, prompt them for their thoughts, or note it to ask later if you risk breaking their flow.

Be flexible

Don't feel the need to squeeze an activity like this in for the sake of it.

Activities like these can be the key to unlock the thoughts of some personalities, but with others you'll have a dynamite dialogue going on. If the conversation is doing all the work, you probably don't need the activity.

Capture

Always take a photo of arrangements and artefacts. Patterns can emerge from these later during analysis, allowing comparison, highlighting similarities and differences.

Reflection

Making the invisible visible is interesting to us, but think about how this experience impacts on the participant.

Laying out a tabletop landscape of actions, decisions, emotions, values and more can reveal aspects of their life they seldom contemplate, resulting in ponderous introspection on their part.

Ask them to reflect: *'How did you feel as you made those choices? What do you think the arrangement says about you?'*

Response to these questions can often even surprise the participant. I've heard people respond with:

'I never realised what an emotionally exhausting experience it was [to buy a home]'

'Seeing that [travel planning process] *I look like quite the control freak. Maybe I am?'*

With triggers for conversation like these, you can be sure the activity was worthwhile.

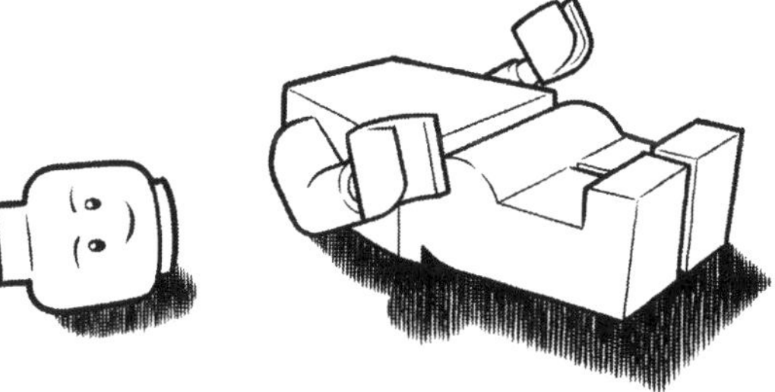

HAPPY ENDINGS

Doorknob moment

Counsellors and therapists recount 'doorknob disclosures', when a client reveals the crux of their issues just as they're leaving the room. Apparently it feels safer for them to share painful truths once they know they can make an exit.

Something similar used to happen in my usability testing days. After an hour of watching someone put a prototype product through its paces, offering luke-warm feedback as they went, I'd then wrap up the session, turn off the cameras and the 'could do better' type comments would spill:

'So, who do they think is going to buy this?'
or *'The designers have gotta go back to basics, don't they?'* or, *'I hope they haven't spent too much money so far'.*

Those comments must have been mooching in their mind for most of the session, but only now did they feel comfortable to let it out.

Now it's me who needs the therapy as I realise I've failed to pick up on these sentiments. Perhaps I didn't build enough rapport or introduce the context of the project well enough for the participant to be fully comfortable. 'Could do better' indeed.

Bring it on

If you're feeling the person is apprehensive or holding back, you could try bringing on the 'doorknob moment' early, to induce a feeling of safety and provide a chance to patch up the hole in your rapport.

A few triggers you can use to suggest the formalities have ended are: *'Well, thanks for that ... great to hear your story...'* (with a rising, 'all done' tone of voice). Shutting your notebook or putting something back in your bag seems to have a similar effect.

Be ready for the person to be somewhat taken aback, but maintain a neutral stance – they've clearly got something to say; they just needed the right conditions in which to say it.

The wrap

When the session really does end, thank the participant by explaining the value of their input to you and the project, and compliment them on how articulate they were.

Around now I sometimes feel a change in atmosphere – a feeling they've just been reminded of the transactional nature of the visit, and they become aware of either the time – they're thinking about their to-do list now you've robbed them of an hour or two, or they've just revealed quite a lot of themselves to a stranger, and you're still in their house.

Either way there can be an awkwardness while you both tread conversational water, exchanging parting pleasantries.

To un-weird this, as I'm packing up my gear, I find myself going back into 'rapport building' mode, as I did upon entering their place. But I'm not opening topics, I'm re-opening them briefly as a way to close the session.

For example, *'So is this a busy time of year in* (insert industry here)?' or I ask for directions to drive on from here.

It's not all awkward, though. Some memorable visits have ended with being invited to stay for dinner, take a tour of the private vintage car collection or go out to a 'ping pong' bar (that was in Berlin, not Bangkok).

From-the-hip summary

You've made your exit, now find somewhere quiet to make a few notes while the echoes of the visit are fresh.

I usually start with a description of the person, their occupation, lifestyle, the things I'd say if someone asked, 'What were they like?'

Alone, or with a partner, list the person's notable attributes, attitudes and behaviours – whatever's stuck in your head, get it out and written down. There are usually a few killer quotes ringing in my ear, too. This is much easier to do as a pair as you can feed off each other's recollections.

Depending on how you're running the project (the amount of time and rigour you can afford), this could be anything from a 5-minute snapshot – a 'cheat sheet' for a full transcript later, or you could take the time now to go over your notes and make a detailed summary.

However much time you allow for this, remember, you'll never have this moment again, and it will quickly be eroded by your experience of the next session, so get your reflections out of your head while you can, even if that means recording an audio file while you drive.

Speaking of recording devices, now let's look in your toolbox ...

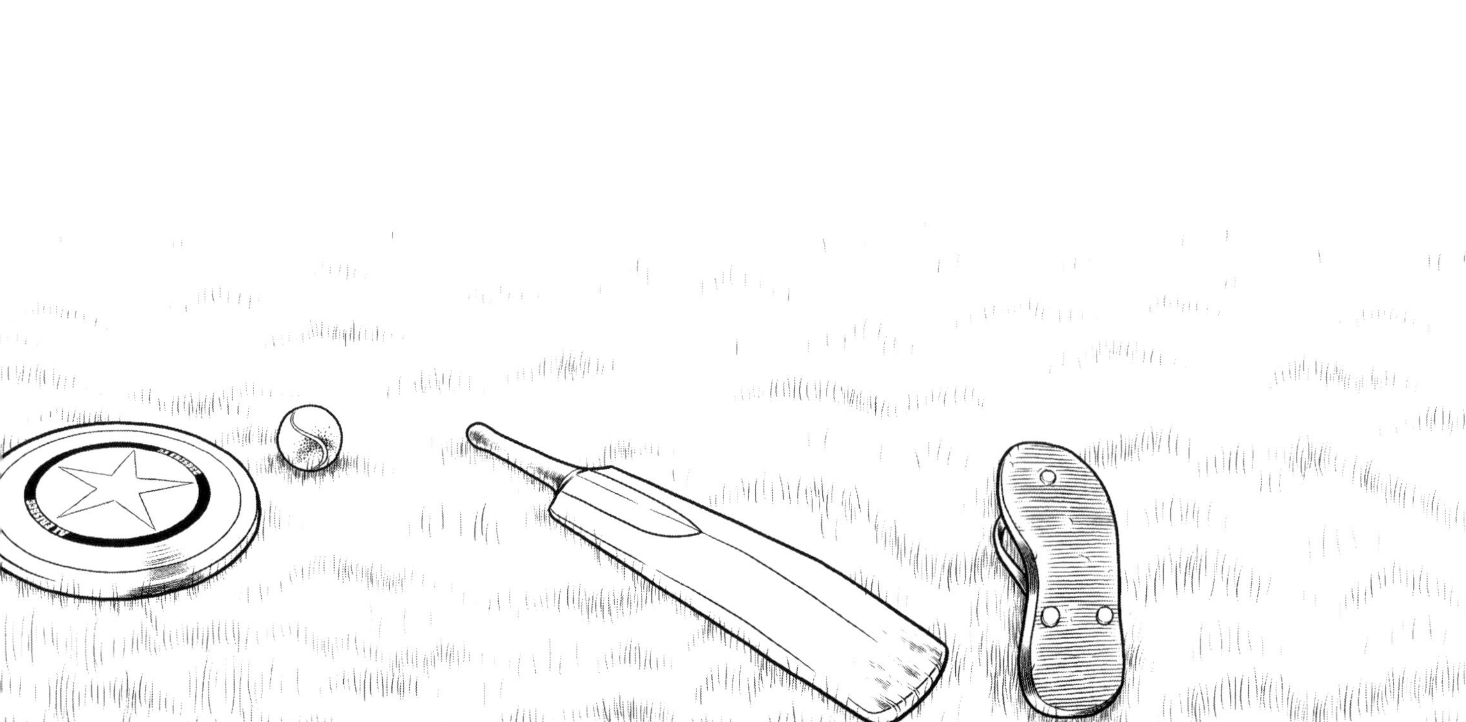

5. TOOLBOX

What to take. Ways to capture

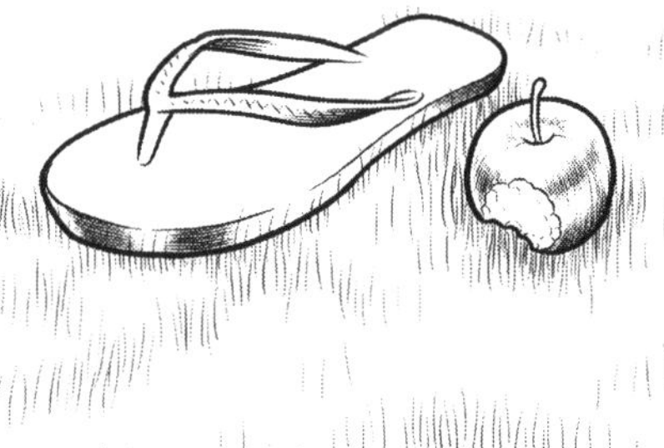

It's you...

Being physically there, with your social skills, senses, and sense of curiosity – you are the most important tool.

Two, Two, One.

Then there's your built-in equipment: your eyes, ears and mouth. The ratio is about right for how much you'll need to use them, too. (Ok, maybe half a mouth would do.)

And time.

When I'm interviewing there's a Mister Miyagi voice in my head saying: *'Nick-san – must go slooow – let flooow'.* (For those of you who don't know, Mister Miyagi was the mentor in *The Karate Kid*. He could catch flies with chopsticks.) Without this voice, I'd feel pressure to extract maximum insight from every minute, rather than taking time to breathe and enjoy the experience.

Even with your senses on, curiosity primed and time locked in – you need gear to capture and record. I'll show you through my kit and explain when, how and why I use each item.

What's in my toolkit?

Every band needs a manager to book the gigs and a roadie to set the stage.

During fieldwork I've rarely had the luxury of a dedicated videographer, and often been operating solo. This means I need to play both manager and roadie roles, but I isolate these activities as much as possible from my role as researcher.

After a few years experimenting with these practicalities, I've curated a toolkit in my backpack, so when I pull up at a field site the roadie can take a back-seat and let me get on with capturing the conversation.

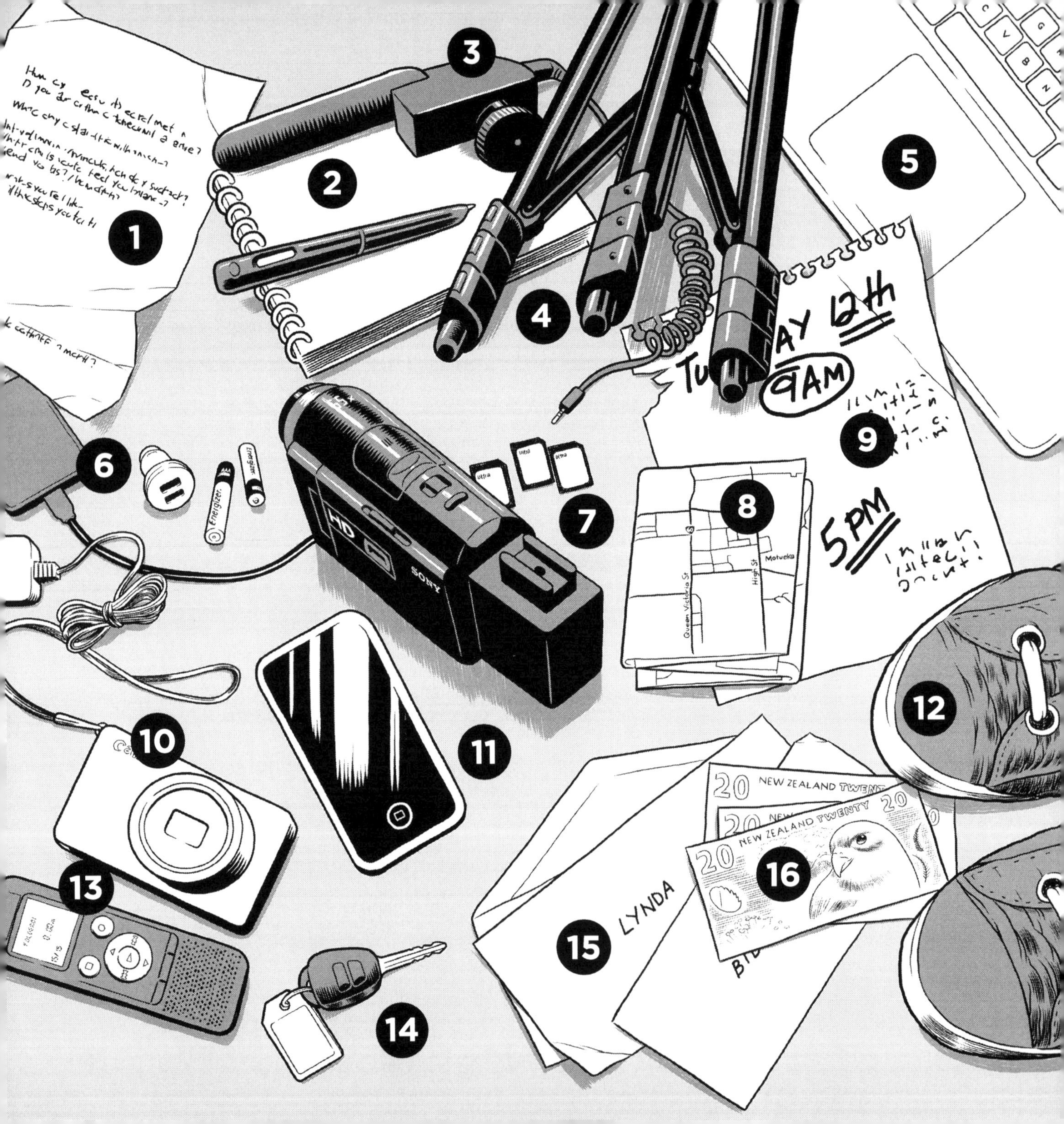
1
2
3
4
5
6
7
8
9
10
11
12
13
14
15
16
AY 12th
9AM
5PM
Energizer
Energizer
Ultra
Ultra
Ultra
HD
SONY
Queen Victoria St
High St
Motueka
NEW ZEALAND TWENTY
NEW ZEALAND TWENTY
20
LYNDA

5. TOOLBOX

1. Discussion guide

A one-page topic list rather than scripted questions.

2. Smart pen

This researcher's best friend. Records every word as you write then plays back the audio from those moments. Like magic, but called Livescribe.

3. Microphone options

Shotgun directional mic. plus wireless lapel mic. for when there's background noise.

4. Tripods

A basic 2–4 footer for working off the floor, and a shorter, bendable tripod – easily shaped into a handle when you need to 'walk and talk' with a participant. Both are fitted with the same quick-release mount for easy switching.

5. Laptop

Used after sessions to type up reflections while they are still fresh. Drive down the road first ... best they don't see you frantically typing about them from behind their curtains.

6. Juice

In-car USB and charging blocks for boosting devices between sessions. Spare batteries and mains chargers. The time you leave them behind will be the time you need them.

7. Video camera

My workhorse is a Sony handycam, pimped with a beast of a battery, quick release mount, capacious data card, shotgun and wireless lapel microphones.

8. Map

Hard copy or online map of the city/area with all the day's participants located. Earns its keep when there's a schedule change and you need to know whether you can actually make it from A–B in the timeframe, and to figure out what neighbourhood you'll be in or near when it's food-o-clock.

9. Schedule

Who, when & where? Usually a pared-down, today-only version, with the full version stashed electronically in case I need phone numbers, etc.

10. Stills camera

Palm-sized and unobtrusive. Quick to boot-up and usable by 'feel' alone (real buttons) with one hand. Passable as a secondary video camera (best if set to the same resolution).

11. Smartphone

Backup/second fiddle for logistics details, maps, image and audio capture, plus alarm for keeping on time, voice to text for brain-dumping thoughts between sessions.

12. Smart/casual clothes

Dress up or down to match the topic, client and neighbourhood. Smart enough to be credible, casual enough to be approachable, and never authoritative. If you're visiting homes, leave the holey socks at yours. Let your partner know the dress code and match it.

13. Audio recorder

A reassuring backup to smartpen and video recordings. Usually the best audio to transcribe from.

14. Rental car

Small & discreet. I try to park out of sight of the address and appear to arrive on foot. ... unless I'm in a rural area, where the 'hobo' interviewer look might arouse suspicion.

15. Paperwork

Some or all of: consent/receipt/image release/NDAs to be signed by participant.

16. Cash incentives

In envelopes for each participant's time and involvement. If you're paying different amounts, name each envelope to avoid awkward moments.

CAPTURE

If you see, hear, think or make it during a visit, it's data.

You'll typically need to bring home a combination of notes, quotes, photos, video, audio, artefacts ...

From the humble note pad to electronic eyes and ears, you need to find the right way to capture data relevant to your project.

A frustrating reality of research is that you won't know which items you'll need until after they've been captured. Look ahead to how you'll use it, so you're not kicking yourself later.

Data takes on two roles as you work through a project:

Raw material: quotes and notes - keeping peoples' voices alive as you find meaning and reach conclusions.

Content: the same photo, artefact, verbatim quote or video clip could well become the material required as deliverables or for debrief activities.

By pre-thinking the shape of the data you need to collect, you can plan how you'll note-take and document in the field. For example, a study focusing on behaviour - observing users interacting with a product or service - will likely require more visual documentation than one centred on attitudes and values.

While it might be tempting to 'record everything' by default, there are advantages to taking a lighter approach, starting with note pad and pen ... (Clipboards are best left in the lab).

Note taking

There are four main types of thing to capture:

WHAT PEOPLE SAID
Quotes, verbatim

WHAT THEY DID
Description of actions, process and tools used

THINGS YOU NOTICE
Observed attitudes/behaviour

QUESTIONS
Things you'd like to ask the participant later

There is no right and wrong way to note-take, but you'll need to balance the need to be:
discreet – minimising impact on the conversation
accessible – if others will need to read your hand-writing
efficient – how scannable are the notes; are they time-stamped to recordings
faithful – being accurate enough that you're not letting the good stuff fall through the cracks

As note-taker it's easier for you to take in the context, noticing things the lead may miss while their focus is on the participant. Telling details, such as a jittering knee under the table when the conversation turns to certain topics, or the unpaid fine on the kitchen bench, can be picked up.

For note-taking, it's hard to go past a note pad and pen, with hand-written notes ranging from 'chicken- scratch' keywords and doodles through to verbatim record of what was said. Typing directly into a laptop or tablet has efficiency on its side, but tends to dehumanise the interaction with the participant.

Pack your poker face

When you take notes, people take notice.

People pay attention to not only what you write but also when and how you write.

You can see this when you review video footage from an interview – every time you look down to the notepad, losing eye contact with the person, they've got their eye on what and how you're writing.

Staying neutral

Note-taking should be a discreet behaviour. If you have a dedicated note-taker, they need to ensure they mute their expressions, not displaying emotion as they jot things down.

EXAMPLE:

GIVING THE GAME AWAY

My client, inventor of a handheld device, sat in on sessions with potential users, where at one stage they compared several working prototypes of his soon-to-be-launched product.

In the sessions I introduced him briefly, by saying: *'My colleague will take some notes'*.

Despite taking notes in silence, his actions ended up giving the game away, because, in the 'doorknob moment' at the end, one participant looked to him and asked: *'Are you the inventor?'*

She explained she could tell by the way he nodded and grimaced, and how vigorously he was writing.

The participant had even figured out which of the prototypes was the favourite by the reactions shown on the inventor's face.

Going solo

If you're a team of two, there's no question about whether to take notes or not, but if you're alone, you'll need to consider how this might impact the flow and quality of the conversation, the atmosphere and power dynamic that taking notes can introduce.

Taking verbatim notes provides a thorough record but is a connection killer. Conversely, going 'commando' by ditching the notepad allows you to focus on the conversation, but increases your reliance on recordings and transcripts later.

So if you're on your own, find a balance between note taking fidelity and conversational quality – minimising impact on the interview while ensuring your notes are intelligible enough to be useful.

A middle ground is to jot only key phrases down, and/or use time codes so you can pin-point these 'golden' moments in your recordings later. The smart pen (#2 from the toolkit) makes this a breeze.

If you know upfront you'll have a chance to review audio recordings or have them transcribed, this can ease fidelity fears, and you can use a lighter note-taking approach.

But, back to the comparative luxury of having (or being) a dedicated scribe:

Avoiding FOMO

You're leading the conversation, valuable dialogue is flowing, but your note-taker's hand is still as a rock.

When working with a rookie scribe, which is common when including clients in the field, such moments will arise, and can be as distracting as they are frustrating.

Pick your moment, but don't be afraid to ask the participant to repeat what they said and suggest directly that the rookie gets it in the bookie.

To set expectations around the level of note-taking detail, it helps to let a newbie note-taker study notes from a previous session.

Sketchnoting

Dorky and official. Ways you don't want to appear – but precisely how I felt – when interviewing patients in a hospital ward.

And because I was feeling clinical and conspicuous jotting down notes while my colleague led the interviews, I pulled out a fat marker to make cartoons of what I was hearing, taking some of the formality away and making the patient more relaxed in what was a vulnerable situation.

It wasn't long before I realised how even the simplest pictures could bring the richness and emotion of these stories to life – especially with a few speech bubbles thrown in.

This may be a tricky approach to try on your own, but if you're the note-taker, and you know you won't be going word for word through your notes, sketching can make for a navigable format to share.

Sharing your sketch-note with the participant gives them a chance to reflect and respond, usually adding to what's there.

A sketch on the project room wall gets a lot of eyeballs and jogs your memory. Beyond a stand-alone artefact, it can be a great prompt for discussion – as you talk others through it, somehow the context and tone of the conversation comes flooding back to you.

Try it yourself.

Here's a 'top 10' from my experience:

1. **Have someone else lead the interview.** This works best if your job is only to listen and capture.

2. **Go BIG – use a large format pad and fat pen.** This prevents you from getting too detailed and, later, makes it easy to read from a distance.

3. **Try to maintain a few seconds 'buffer'** between what you're hearing and what you're drawing.

4. **Share your doodle with the participant,** especially if they're distracted by it. They'll soon get back to the conversation.

5. **Use visual metaphors,** for example, if the subject is looking for something, draw binoculars, magnifying glass, map or compass.

6. **Pepper the notes with punchy verbatim quotes** using speech or thought bubbles to carry their voice.

7. **Use a couple of sizes or styles of text** to indicate degrees of strength of a comment or specific themes. I use lower case for quotes, for example.

8. **Talk the participant through the sketch** at the end of the interview. They'll be pleased to see what all the scribbling has been about.

9. **Ask for comment.** 'What else would you add?' The person might make corrections or add further texture to the story, to be added on the spot.

10. **Sit away from the microphone** if you're recording – felt-tip markers make quite a racket when you're going full-tilt.

Filming

If you can – film.

While your eyes and ears are designed for the job, your 'computer' they're hooked up to can't process the amount of data passing through them to capture it all.

For a humbling lesson in how much dialogue you miss during a session, compare your notes from a field visit to a transcript of what was actually said. Reviewing video easily doubles what you missed – all the visual cues, non-verbals and mannerisms, as well as the contextual details.

This, plus the impact of video when sharing your work, makes film an essential medium for almost every project.

Using video serves three purposes:

1. Video as data

Rich and immersive, it provides the most complete set of data to work from during analysis. Going back to moments in the footage from a session brings the context and atmosphere flooding back, triggering your senses and associated feelings.
Audio + photos can get you some of the way there, but video will always be king.

2. Video as medium

Edited fieldwork footage is an engaging medium to support your insights, and can be compelling enough to inspire teams into action.

With a little (ok, a lot of) editing effort, you can have the customer and their context paint their own picture, tell their story and do the convincing for you.

... and in my experience the more you use video, the more you get of the latter.

3. Video as record

Clients will occasionally ask for the footage as a record, but in my experience few will ever actually view it (particularly if you've done a great job of pulling together a highlight reel).

Make sure you have proper participant consent for storage (and all types of use) to comply with data protection law. Be transparent with participants and hold up your obligations.

So as data, a medium or just an insurance policy, a good default is to film and record sessions.

There are a few exceptions to using video, for example, if;

- there's a legal, ethical or moral reason not to
- it doesn't feel right given the subject matter or context
- only selecting people who agree to be filmed might bias the sample
- when the project is so brutally time-constrained that there's no chance the footage will be viewed – even as a data source

Filming: Overheads

Before you grab the camera gear, be aware of the overheads filming carries during and after fieldwork.

During sessions:

Oh! but my hair's a total mess

So, who exactly will see this?

This better not end up on YouTube!

But you said you'd take notes?

The sight of a camera can present a physical reminder of the commercial nature of the visit – even make people recoil at the intrusion and threat to privacy.

These responses can be reduced to almost zero by giving people time to process it in advance.

Always gain permission during recruitment, then again by having them read and sign a consent form before you get the camera out.

Be alert for the raised eyebrow or comment as you're setting up the camera. There are times people squirm, become self-conscious and need assurance, so, acknowledge and address their concerns.

Be honest, confident yet casual, but not glib. Sure, use your charm to tell them their hair looks fine, but don't brush their concerns off or downplay them.

I often stress how useful it is as a memory jogger for me: 'After a day or two of these interviews, it can become a bit of a blur, so it really helps if I can go back and recall things just as you said it.'

'Don't point that thing at me!'
If your explanation and assurance isn't cutting it, ask for a compromise of audio plus a few photos.

Another approach is to ask (again) at the tail end of the visit. Their experience of the session should have muted their concerns and their guard will be down. You'll need to judge their openness to this, but you could ask whether they'd consider making a handful of key statements or 'replays' of moments during the session for the camera.

Mental bandwidth
You're in the vital first few minutes of a visit. Brick-by-brick you're building the foundation of rapport the interview will rely on. Then, for just 20 seconds, you need to turn your thoughts to setting up and checking your recording gear. Unless you're an incredible multi-tasker, an awkward silence ensues as all the attention goes from them onto your kit.

At this moment your note-taker should know to keep the conversation flowing – or even tackle the setup discretely while you do – but if you're alone, you'll need to battle through any awkwardness until you're 100 per cent sure the camera set-up is watertight. Without this confidence a gremlin of doubt will be tapping on your shoulder, distracting your attention during the session.

Do I have enough space on my memory card?

Will 40% battery last an hour?

Did I press record twice by accident?

All your best efforts can be scuppered if batteries run dry, memory cards max out, or the person moves partially out of shot – not to mention the participant's dog mistaking your rubbery tripod legs for a chewing toy.

You can plan for those first two, but probably best not to use your tripod to tenderize your steak the night before the fieldwork.

Filming: Overheads

After the sessions

Handling your precious video footage can become a time thief, snaffling away hours or days, usually from the vulnerable tail end of your project – time you'll need to budget for.

Exactly how much time depends on how you plan to use your footage:

Data analysis
If it's a core part of your analysis – you're reviewing every moment and mannerism, transcribing (and perhaps making a highlight reel) as you go. Allow two to three hours to review every hour of footage.

Insight support
If you're using notes or transcripts for analysis and just using the video to support these findings, the speediest way is to cherry-pick selected moments, located by time-codes from your notes. Working this way you could build a short highlight reel in a day.

Narrative building
If you're editing a cohesive story with a compelling narrative down from 20+ hours of footage, or compiling several clips to represent individual themes, get ready for your inner Spielberg to appear – gobbling up several days.

Wide, or deep?

With the weight of all that footage, and a fixed window of editing time, you'll need to be thinking, *'How can the footage best support the insights for the project/audience?'*

This usually means going wide (lightly across all the footage) or deep (narrowing down to a defined subset).

WIDE:

Going for volume with a 'vox-pop' style clip, with a quantity of 'talking heads', contexts and behaviours. Valuable for supporting findings when you need to convey how prevalent or diverse they are across your sample.

Practically speaking, this means dealing with a large amount of footage, relying heavily on your notes, knowing where to look to 'harvest' those select moments.

This is where time-coding your notes in the field pays you back in hours of edit time.

DEEP:

Focusing on building narrative around individual experiences, selecting a subset (even just a couple of individuals from the sample) and reviewing a manageable amount of footage and stills more thoroughly, allowing time to frame and tell their story.

You need to choose participants who represent findings well, challenge thoughts and have contrasting attitudes/behaviours.

This approach relies on you having the trust of your audience – that you're not influencing the insights through the people you select – so it's worth involving a key stakeholder in the rationale behind who to include.

Foolproof filming

Choosing a video camera is full of trade-offs, but the decision is easy once you know what you're willing to compromise on and what you're not.

You can get results from all of: Gopro/action camera, Smartphone, Point&shoot, DSLR, Handycam etc. ... but trade-offs usually lie between these factors:

Size/form
Will it be intimidating or too 'in your face'?

Battery life
Will it last for the length of a session?

Storage
How much space can it handle? Which type of memory cards? Ease of transfer?

Viewfinder
How easy is it to check the framing of the shot, light, focus?

Microphone options
Will it accept an external lapel microphone? What about a wireless one?

Zoom
Can you crop or widen the shot without moving the camera or fussing with controls?

Accessories for smartphones and action cams are abundant but after trying all of the types above, **here's why I go with a handycam almost every time:**

All day battery
A beasty brick provides clip-on juice for around eight hours of filming. This means never thinking about battery levels, charging or changing, and only one battery to charge overnight.

Microphone options
No amount of visual resolution will make up for patchy audio. There will be situations where a patchy recording is as good as you can get with a built-in mic., such as when I interviewed someone in a squash club, to the backdrop of balls 'bonking' off glass and the grunts of players battling it out. Or in a hushed hospital ward – patients whispering their medical memoirs so as not to be heard through paper-thin curtains.

Handycams have accessory mounts that allow you to use mics built for these scenarios. If there's a fairly steady background noise, it's worth using a 'shotgun' mic. These focus the microphone directly on whoever's in front of the camera, leaving just enough of the background sound to add atmosphere.

When the background noise is more invasive (in a cafe a shotgun mic can be no match for a coffee grinder at 1500 rpm) or if the person is whispering, you'll pick it all up with a 'lapel' mic.

The best of these are wireless and small enough to clip onto the person's collar. Also good when following someone around their home, factory, driving or in the street.

Flip-out viewfinder.
Nothing reminds the participant they are being filmed like a fumble with the camera or leaning around to check the framing of the shot. A flip-out viewfinder reduces this to a quick glance.

Zoom.
Wide-angle action cameras are great if you're up close or opposite someone at a kitchen table, but when you're half a room away they can shrink your subject in a fish-eye effect. Handycams (and others) let you zoom right on in. This (along with the mic options) means you can deliberately place the camera further from the participant (less intrusive) and still have a great shot with audio to match.

Snapshot.
Some video cameras have a physical 'snapshot' button to fire off stills while shooting. Perfect when someone's demonstrating how they do something.

Ace of face.
I realised face detection was useful when I discovered my handycam takes a still photo every time a participant smiles. This means automatically snapping sometimes dozens of shots of candid moments I could never capture with a still camera. A super useful set of mugshots for your documentation later.

Custom capture

Remaining discreet and unobtrusive sometimes requires improvisation, attaching cameras to objects or even yourself in order to capture the action.

In a street or retail environment a small video camera strapped to a shoulder bag or cut away into a paper coffee cup will barely draw attention compared to a hand-held one.

Watching people interact with mobile devices can reveal a lot about their intention and attention but can test the laws of personal space. When you need to be close to the action like this, but don't want to influence the person's behaviour, try mounting a camera to the device using a hacked selfie-stick or a bent coat-hanger and a clamp.

After several iterations of this I designed and commercialised 'Mr. Tappy', a product purpose-built for just this job - capturing how people interact with mobile devices. He's since been attached to wheelchairs, car dashboards, fish-finders and shopping carts in order to film people tapping and swiping.

Film footage may be your most compelling evidence, so it's worth going to lengths to capture the moment from the user's perspective.

Quickdraw

Pop, click, fiddle, flip ... goes the 'dance' as you faff with setting up your camera gear.

Big budget research projects might have the luxury of a videographer who will keep this discreet, or you might have a partner to handle this for you, but when you're setting up alone with a patter of small-talk to keep up, fumbling with your gear can be a rapport-breaker.

I try to eliminate the fumbles through the way I prepare and carry my kit. Arranging everything I need in a single box, set up becomes a matter of attaching the camera to the tripod, powering up, framing the shot and hitting record, as opposed to a rummaging treasure hunt through every compartment of my bag.

Audio

Filming or not, I'll make an audio recording of the session.

An audio track can be a:

- less intrusive option than video, especially in sensitive contexts
- back-up for the inevitable camera fail
- lighter way to share the session with your team (MB rather than GB file sizes)
- faster way to get audio to a transcription service (than video)
- second (sometimes higher quality) audio track for video
- great accompaniment to still photos. Artefact and environmental shots with the participant's voice-over can make for a very watchable alternative to full video

I double-down on my smartpen with a digital voice recorder, being careful to synch the start times so the time-codes match later.

If the session is conducted in another language, add a second recorder (held in the translator's hand) for a high-quality recording of the translation from which to make a transcript should you need it.

Stills

Photos are an essential and powerful artefact from field visits. They'll jog your memory, illustrate what you saw, and even reveal aspects you hadn't noticed in the moment, from your field visit. They also make for a compelling story-telling medium, especially when combined with audio.

In an ideal world you'll have all your attention on the participant, and a well-briefed partner (your note-taker) behind the lens. Discuss the type and quantity of shots required: a variety of wide context shots, through to artefacts, activity and candid moments.

Choice of camera is personal, but erring towards the discreet will reduce the paparazzi effect. Smartphone cameras score well here, but a pocket-able point & shoot requires less attention and lets you fire one-handed without looking.

Shot list

If you're working alone, every time you snap a photo is an interrupt in your engagement or connection with the person. Between what the participant demonstrates, and objects and artefacts, you will miss things.

Rather than interrupt the flow, make a 'shot list' of things you'd like to capture at the end of the session. As you're winding up, ask the participant to re-enact a moment from the session, pose in a certain context or take a photograph of a collection of objects.

For example, *'Could I grab a shot of you sitting out there on the porch with your ipad, in what you said was your favourite chair?'*

It may sound contrived, but these, and a couple of mugshots in context with audio overlaid describing their attitude or behaviour, can rival video, plus it allows you to focus and observe more during the visit.

Overkill

While you'll almost always wish you had more photos, there's a risk of overdoing it as far as the participant is concerned.

Defuse the thought you're overstepping the mark by politely asking permission and explaining the relevance of the types of photos you're taking early on in the visit. If you feel you need to explain why you're taking the shot, ask yourself whether it's really required.

Bookends

In the same way a film-maker uses a 'clapper board', I take a photo of my hand just before/after each visit. This proves handy later when organising hundreds of shots according to which visit they were from.

MAKING SENSE

Analysis of data & synthesis of findings

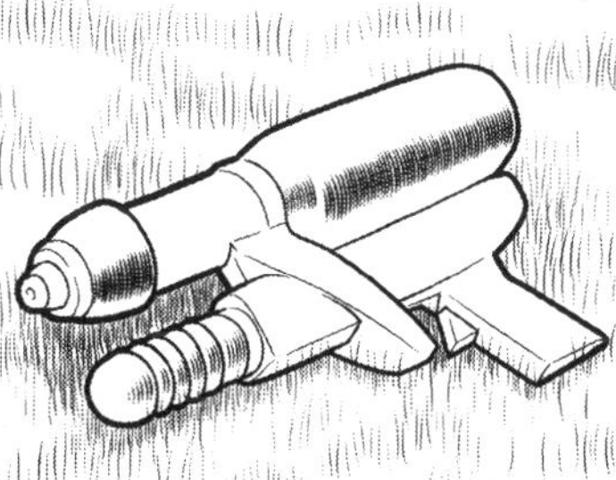

Unpacking

James, my gardener friend, never visits without casting a critical eye over my compost heap. He's somewhat obsessed by the stuff – says I need to soak it, turn it over, mix it, let it breathe – and he promises the goodness will come with time.

It pays to take a similarly organic approach to analysing your data. Some of the 'composting' is already happening in your mind, but you need to take the time to collate, extract and filter through the data to make sense of it. Then you'll need to use your instincts to best synthesise what you've learned, and why it's important.

It's an 'expand to fit' activity, which can take anywhere from an afternoon to days on end. At the lighter end, you could come away with a 'top ten' from each interview from your summary notes and start looking for common threads.

At the rigorous end, you'll serve a week-long sentence in a prison of pastel squares – pushing sticky-notes and your sanity through several thresholds of 'are we there yet?'

You'll find your happy medium – this is a process you need to feel your way through. But, having served time doing both lighter and rigorous, I'll go over the common components of a relatively thorough approach, so you can scale back to suit your own time.

Start with the people

Some characters leave more of an impression than others, but it's too early to start calling favourites until you've emerged from the upcoming fog.

Stick your post-session summary notes up on a wall, then print and pin a mugshot of the person to each, creating an at-a-glance profile. After a week or more of back-to-back interviews this is a visual walk down memory lane.

Name and number each profile sheet. Your data and quotes will be numbered, too, so this makes it possible for a visitor to figure who said what, even if you're not there to relive the moment. Think of this as a kind of 'legend' to the walls of data you're about to populate.

Transcribing

For time-constrained projects, notes and quotes taken during a session may be the limit of your data. Going deeper means revisiting the dialogue and transcribing from your recordings. It's time consuming, but invaluable, and is the raw material of analysis.

From each interview, transcribe each notable observation and/or verbatim onto a sticky note.

Put the number of the interview in the corner, so later it's possible to spot patterns where the same people show up in certain themes and to reference back to your numbered mugshots on the wall. Your signal-to-noise ratio will vary between interviews, so you could end up with 20–50 stickies from an hour of recording.

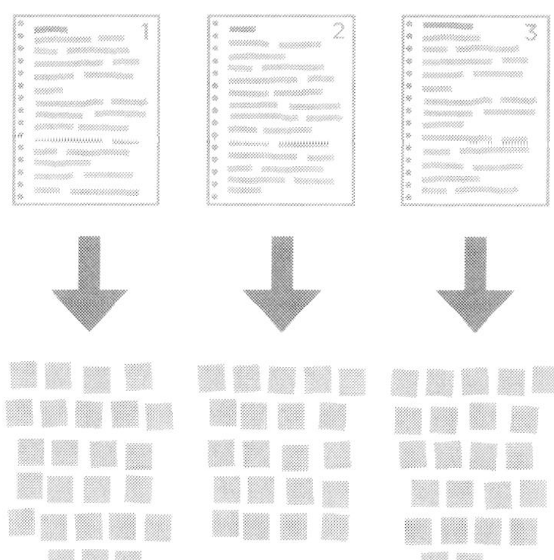

Reviewing footage or audio recordings minute-by minute sounds painstaking, but it's an investment in the quality of the work to follow.

Reviewing from video is the most thorough way to transcribe your sessions. As well as seeing what people are doing, you'll clock all those subtle non-verbals (like an inhale between the teeth before making a statement), which are harder to pick from audio. If you're fairly confident of the 'magic moments', you could also be pulling video clips for your highlight reel as you go, or just adding the time code to help pin-point these, come editing time.

There are overnight transcription services, which charge a per-minute rate to turn your audio files into a word doc. These can be a time saver, but come at the cost of your deeper immersion and reflection with the data.

As tempting as it is to outsource this, doing your own transcription is an often overlooked way to hone your skills. It holds a mirror up to your technique; you can review your interview style warts and all, and critically evaluate how your questions and timing work – or don't – all while getting the job done.

To affinity and beyond

Analysis is a fluid process, with indistinct phases. The 'end' can seem elusive, there's no definable halfway point, but the start is always the same: a pile of data.

The feeling during the process is the same too: a nebulous sense of being lost or even drowning.

Whilst an immersive experience, analysis requires you to zoom in and out of the data, adding layers of definition and meaning as you go, eventually you emerge with clarity.

For now, though, it's time to embrace the ambiguity, because nobody is better placed to make sense of this data than you, and while it's possible to forge ahead alone, it's quicker, more conclusive and fun when accompanied by a partner who was part of the fieldwork.

We'll use a hypothetical travel planning project to walk through the process, taking typical steps in a fairly common order.

EXAMPLE PROJECT:

TRAVEL PLANNING

Your client is an airline looking to understand how frequent leisure travellers plan and book their holidays.

They have a solid understanding of how flights are booked, but want to learn about the wider process, with a focus on planning and booking accommodation. It's an area they are looking at moving into.

You and a colleague carefully selected and interviewed 15 travellers at various stages of trip planning.

Each traveller demonstrated their planning approach and experience relating to a recent or upcoming trip.

Dive into the data

> You've unpacked your data and are set to make sense of it all.

You have:

- participant snapshots – summary and photo from each session
- hundreds of sticky notes with quotes and observations. One pile per field visit, numbered by session
- blank sticky notes and markers
- a blank, smooth wall or window space (>2m long)
- uninterrupted time
- focus

1. Starting points

To get the ball rolling, write fresh sticky notes for 5–10 key starting categories, e.g. 'inspiration', 'tools', 'ratings & reviews' etc.
Space these out at eye level along the wall. Don't be precious about naming; these are short-term parking to group your data under until they find a more considered home.

2. Introductions

Take one participant snapshot each, introducing them by describing their attributes out loud. This will jog your memory, bring the person into the room, and help anchor you back to the context in which each of the quotes or observations were made.

3. Grouping

Take turns to read your pile of sticky-notes aloud, one-by-one, as you place them on the wall under a category to form groups.

When it's not obvious which group a note fits within, discuss whether it's the start of a new group, or it belongs in two groups and you need to write a duplicate. E.g.: 'I check the Trip Advisor reviews, then contact the hotel direct to see what they can offer' might fit within Reviews, but also kick off a new group called Direct Booking.

> Your data is beginning to fall into themes.

4. Grow the web

Once you have a few dozen notes on the wall, your 'starting point' categories might become too broad, need renaming or have to break into sub-groups.

As you work through each participant's notes, continue to make new group or sub-group names until you've found homes for almost all your stickies.

Some groups will have two notes, others 22, but prevalence doesn't equal significance - a single note may carry as much weight as a handful.

Park random notes off to the side, they may find a place later (or never).

Now you're standing in front of a loosely arranged map of your data. You share an understanding of what's on the wall and where, but the group names and their 'footprint' are subject to change.

5. Boiling the ocean

Focusing on one group at a time, pass the contents through a more critical filter. Scan each note in the group to interrogate:

- Does it belong?
- How well does the name of the group describe the contents?
- Do some of these notes also belong elsewhere?
- Is there a sub-group to be formed?

Smaller groups may be merged, larger groups may be broken into sub-groups. New groups will form. As these consolidate and proliferate, give them more descriptive names, each time making a new sticky note. E.g. 'Reviews' breaks down into 'Reviews as a decision-making tool', 'Lack of trust in reviews', 'Motivation to submit a review'.

6. Zooming out

Looking at the entire data set, specifically the group descriptions, arrange the groups into a configuration which best reflects how they relate to each other.

In our travel example: Travel blogs, Word of mouth and Social media might all be moved to fall together under 'Inspiration'.

If you have an unwieldy quantity of notes, make a duplicate set of the group title sticky notes to arrange separately on an adjacent surface, re-ordering the main wall to match afterwards.

Now you have a more refined set of themes arranged in a way which shows how these relate to each other.

7. Voice and meaning

With your pattern-spotting engine purring, look at each group, focusing on the participant numbers in the corners of each note.

- Is one group populated with just two or three people?
- Do certain people dominate several related categories?
- What do they have in common?

Refer to your participant profiles on the wall – to identify the 'who' behind the 'what'. This will help you spot behaviours common or unique to certain mindsets, customer types, etc., and highlight potential on-the-edge cases – where you have just one voice filling a category of their own – so you can determine how much weight to apply to that finding.

Adjust the descriptions of the groups to suit. E.g., Direct booking might become 'Groups and families booking multiple rooms prefer to book directly with hotels'.

8. Adding voices

Up to this point, you've described the themes based on your interpretation. Now it's time to add the customer's voice, and what it means to them.

Choose a quote from each group, which best captures or summarises the theme in their words. Alternatively, you could paraphrase while maintaining their voice:
'Bad reviews tell me which places to avoid'; 'I use the reviews to make a shortlist'; 'Reviews help me see through the marketing hype'.

Position these with your group names as headlines to represent the sentiment of the individuals in that group.

Now your themes can be read according to whom they represent, in their own terms, as well as yours.

9. Brass tacks

Turn your theme names into statements of truth to concisely represent what you discovered, like: 'Travellers easily become overwhelmed by choice' or 'Travellers seek social validation from reviews'.

There's no room for ambiguity here. Play the devil's advocate or invite a colleague who wasn't part of the fieldwork to do this, critiquing each finding. Does it speak for all customers, just certain types, or only in certain situations? Adjust each statement until it withstands tyre-kicking.

Language matters. Be careful using absolute terms such as all/none, always/never, unless you are certain this would apply to a wider sample.

Now you have a set of concise findings you can stand by, accompanied by customers' voices.

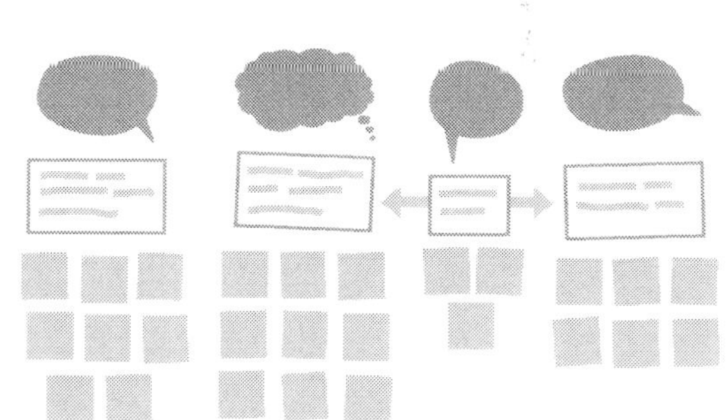

10. Narrative

Zooming out from the data again, draw further links and relationships between your findings to reveal the bigger story they tell.

Arrange these (perhaps on another blank surface) in a way that lets you join dots, make connections and spot conflicts. Three or four findings might belong together; some might feed into another. Some relate to attitudes, emotions and behaviours. Some attitudes might map directly to behaviours. Some findings may be underpinned by values and beliefs.

Write new sticky notes, draw lines, arrows etc between them to describe connections, conflicts and relationships and what they mean in your customer's world. Use the customer's voice where you can to annotate these.

For example, a group of findings around 'triggers to travel', and another around 'influences' might both feed into a decision on their destination. 'Reviews' might be one of those influences: 'Travellers begin using ratings and reviews to evaluate options, then use them to shortcut their decision-making'.

11. Evidence

Carefully considered insights will form the backbone for a report, poster or presentation, and will need to be backed up by data. Data which adds a human element.

For each insight, find statements in the user's voice to represent it, noting the participant's name, age and customer type if relevant. Using two or three quotes helps reveal nuances and demonstrates the finding isn't a response to just a single voice.

EXAMPLE INSIGHT

VOICE OF CUSTOMER

I love choice, but not making choices

FINDINGS

Overwhelmed by accommodation options and marketing, travellers rely on ratings and reviews to short-cut their decision.

EVIDENCE

Straight away I can see the guest photos look as good as the hotel website, so that's a contender!

MARTIA, 28 YRS

Because these reviews aren't marketing hype, you trust it more so it makes an easier decision

SAM, 49 YRS

Knocking out everything below a 4-star makes the decision much easier for us

DINA, 36 YEARS

By bringing each finding to a point of clarity, and with time spent on how they relate to each other, your insights are synthesised and ready to become part of something greater.

7. OUTPUTS & OUTCOMES

Shaping & positioning your learnings to make an impact

Form follows insight

Let the needs of your audience shape your output.

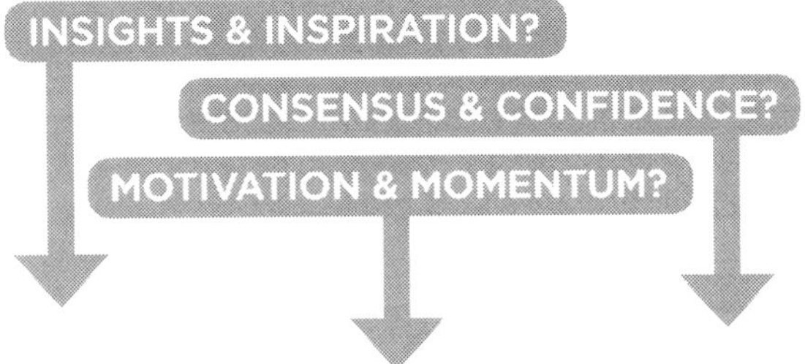

An understanding of your client's position and the decisions they're facing should inform your choice of format, priority of content, tone of voice, level of detail, etc., to maximise the relevance and impact of your findings.

Limiting yourself to a single, pre-agreed or boilerplate format can see you miss the mark in a similar way to product companies who start with a technology or solution in mind, then try to make it fit the customer. When a client suggests a specific output from the start, try to rewind a few steps to get to the 'why?' behind the 'what?' Encourage conversation about deliverables in terms of verbs. Ask 'what will the output do for the team? Is it to challenge, convince or inspire?'

This dialogue helps you understand what the client needs, rather than what they've asked for. It helps them remain open, rather than locking in to a particular end point, and lets you remain responsive to their reactions to challenges and opportunities the findings reveal.

Start with quality

The quality and value of your work will be determined by the clarity of thought behind it.

When expressed through words, often it's a case of fewer = better.

Work and re-work every finding and insight, until it concisely reflects what you've learned and what this means to the business.

Go for walks. Sleep on it. Edit.

Have a colleague once-removed from the project review your work, to ensure it won't leave people wondering or be misinterpreted.

Check the level of detail. Every point you add stretches your audience's attention a little thinner.

Options & formats

With your insights boiled to their essence, you're a production job away from creating something to inspire and inform your audience. This could range from a standalone document to a facilitated experience, and many others in between.

Report or slide deck.
The classic, most expected format for sharing your insights.

Typical structure is to describe:
Why: Project objectives, research and business questions
What: Approach, method, activities
Who: Sample size, location, demographics, recruitment criteria

Then tell the story of what you discovered. For our travel planning example, you might go linear, working through phases of an experience: starting with a traveller's context and mindset, then covering inspiration and information sources, before moving into comparing and deciding on providers etc.

This is narrative-building, and a creative decision, but whatever shape it takes, the content should be informed by your experience of the customer's world and underpinned by evidence from it. Add layers of evidence - quotes, photos, illustrations, to ground your insights in reality.

Every insight should be framed by context, supported by the voice of the customer and describe the challenge or opportunity it presents.

Beyond a traditional report, variations and combinations of all the following are useful:

Journey maps.
Visually illustrating the experience (highs, lows, layers, phases and elements) of interacting with a product or service along a timeline.

Personas.
Profiles of archetypal customers, representing their attributes, needs, goals and the challenges and opportunities they present.

Jobs to be done.
Laser-focused analysis of what the customer wants to achieve and why.

Storyboards.
Describing scenarios of use, step-by-step. i.e., 'Day in the life'.

Video highlights.
Usually edited into themes to support key findings or to profile customer types.

Workshops.
Facilitated activities exposing teams to curated materials, encouraging individual and collective response, leading towards their own conclusions.

Hybrid outputs.
Some of the most successful outputs I've seen are mixtures - drawing elements from those listed above - bespoke to the needs of the project. Experiment by cherry-picking components which work for where your team is at, and where they need to be.

On the next pages are a couple of staples I keep coming back to, for the impact they bring. I'll talk through why I think they work, and how you can try them.

Get visual

Visuals can extend beyond their initial graphic impact to tell stories, build context, explain relationships and show processes.

As part of a final deliverable – and particularly in workshop situations – they can be absorbed in a fraction of the time it takes to read a report. They also have shelf life, earning their share of viewings when up on the wall in the corridor, kitchen or team space.

STEP BY STEP

The following page shows the steps I usually take to visualise research findings – an example from a hospital-ward design project, exploring patient experience in shared versus single rooms.

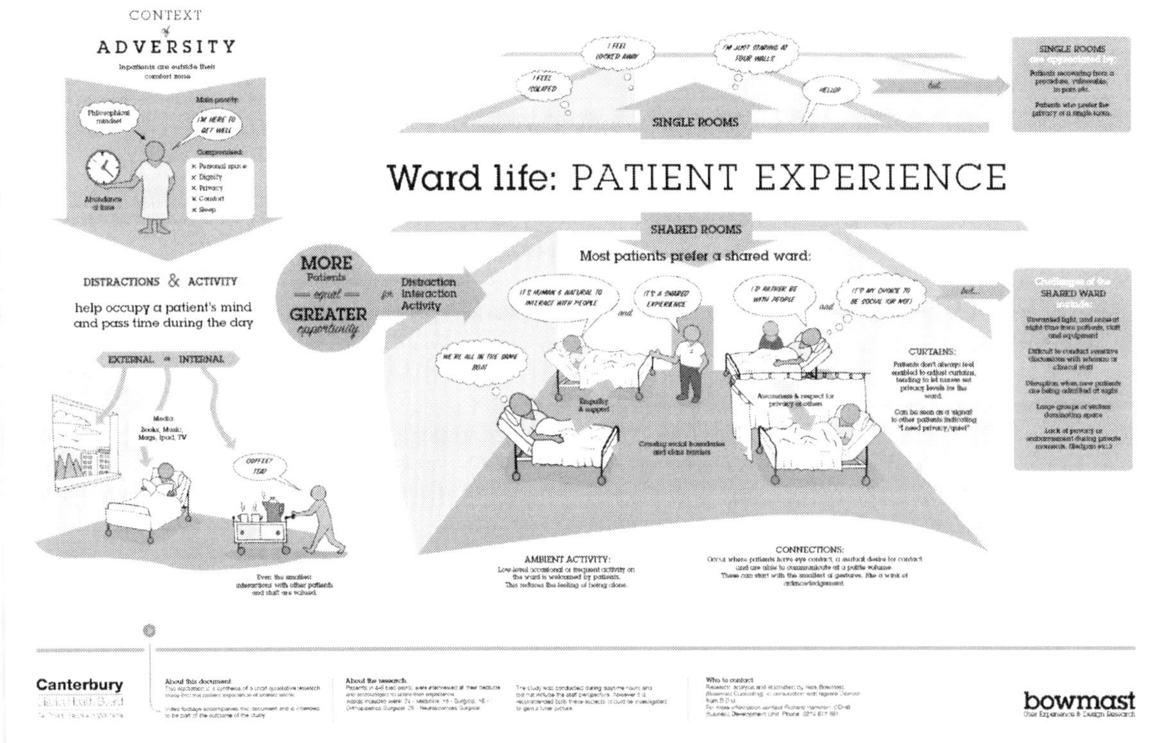

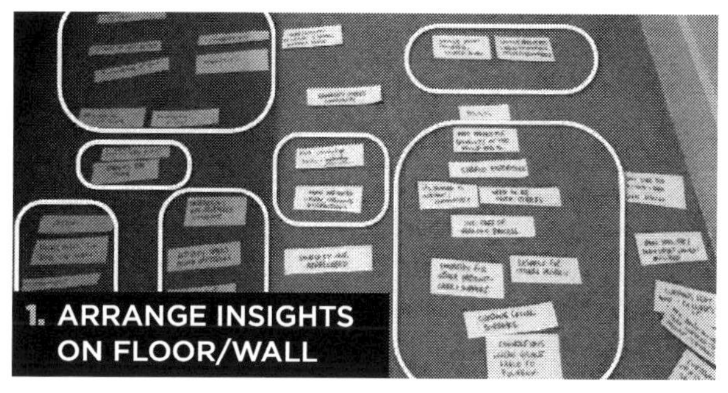

1. ARRANGE INSIGHTS ON FLOOR/WALL

2. THEN ON PAPER

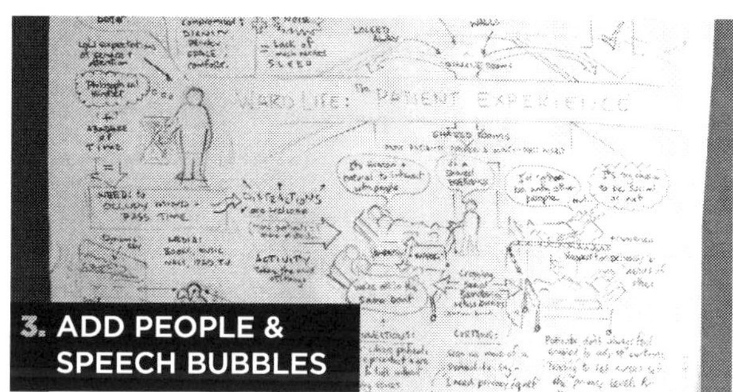

3. ADD PEOPLE & SPEECH BUBBLES

4. FETCH OR SKETCH PEOPLE & PROPS

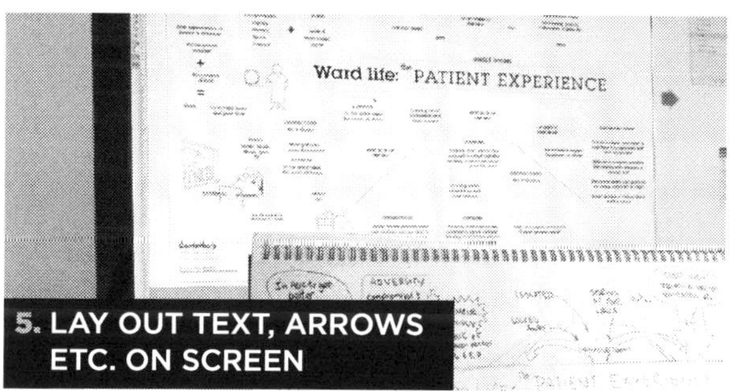

5. LAY OUT TEXT, ARROWS ETC. ON SCREEN

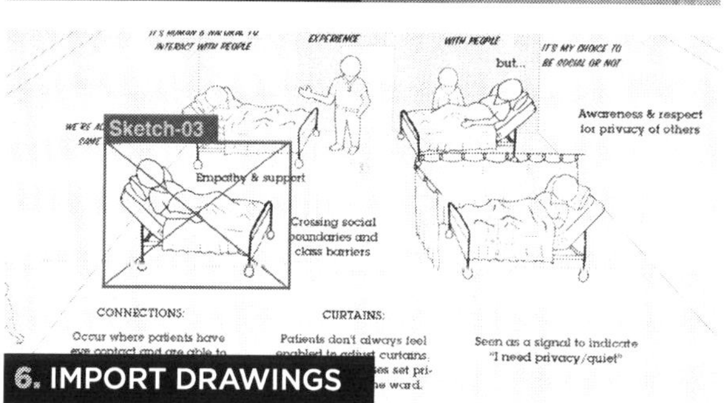

6. IMPORT DRAWINGS

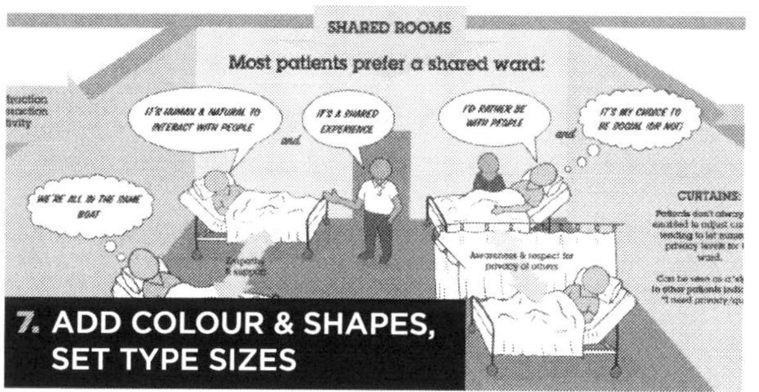

7. ADD COLOUR & SHAPES, SET TYPE SIZES

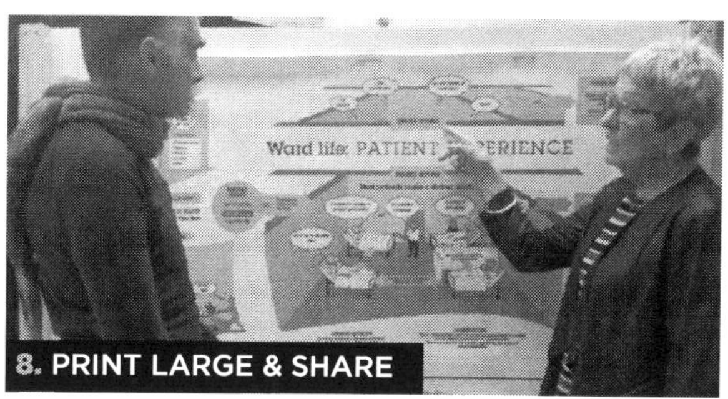

8. PRINT LARGE & SHARE

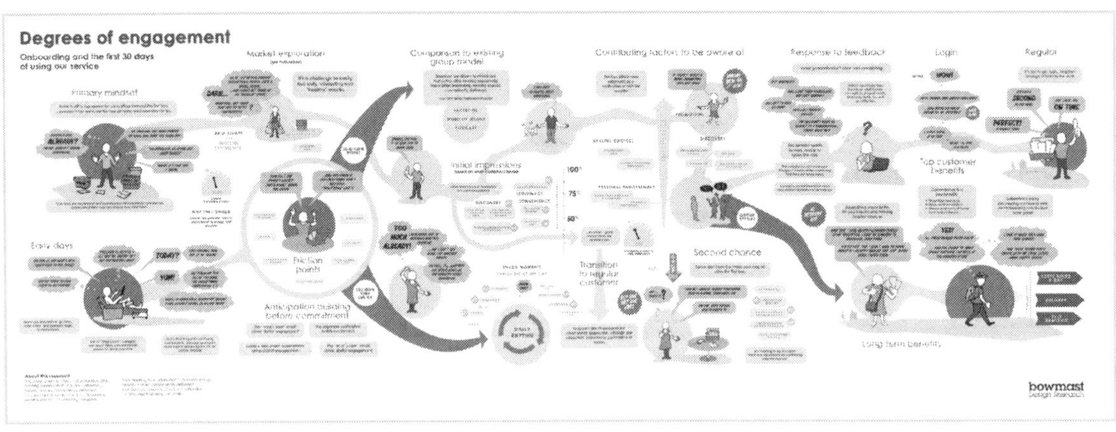
Degrees of engagement
Onboarding and the first 30 days of using our service
Market exploration
Comparison to existing group model
Contributing factors to be aware of
Response to feedback
Login
Regular
Primary mindset
Initial impressions
Friction points
Anticipation building before commitment
Early days
Transition to regular customer
Second chance
Top customer benefits
Long term benefits
100%
75%
50%
bowmast
Design Research

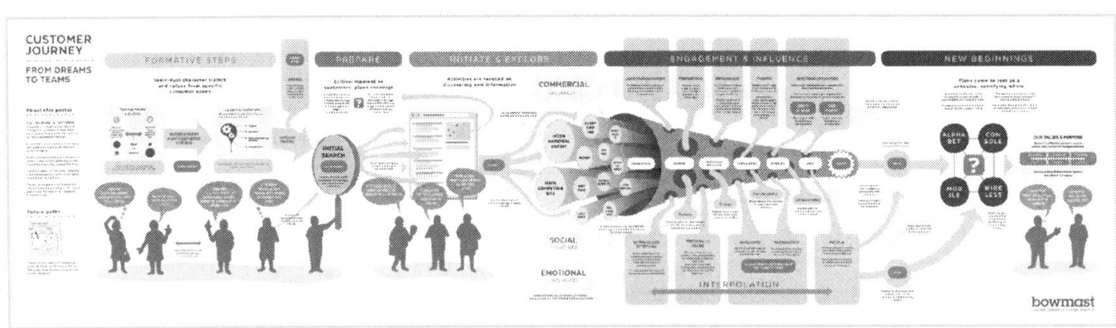
CUSTOMER JOURNEY
FROM DREAMS TO TEAMS
FORMATIVE STEPS
PREPARE
INITIATE & EXPLORE
ENGAGEMENT & INFLUENCE
NEW BEGINNINGS
COMMERCIAL
SOCIAL
EMOTIONAL
INITIAL SEARCH
ALPHA BET
CON SOLE
MOB ILE
WIRE LESS
INTERPOLATION
bowmast

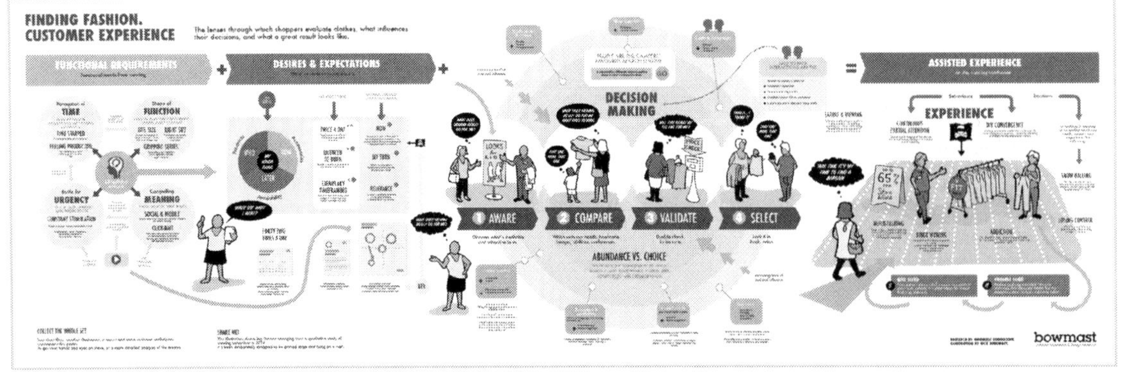
FINDING FASHION.
CUSTOMER EXPERIENCE
The lenses through which shoppers evaluate clothes, what influences their decisions, and what a great result looks like.
FUNCTIONAL REQUIREMENTS
DESIRES & EXPECTATIONS
ASSISTED EXPERIENCE
TIME
FUNCTION
URGENCY
MEANING
DECISION MAKING
1 AWARE
2 COMPARE
3 VALIDATE
4 SELECT
ABUNDANCE VS. CHOICE
EXPERIENCE
65%
bowmast

Eight top tips for visualising insights

1. Metaphor

Rabbit in the headlights. Hot knife through butter. Elephant in the room.

Metaphors, similes and analogies are effective ways to help your audience view something new through a familiar lens. Using similar and easy-to-identify components provides a relatable comparison, short-cutting their thinking.

This can also be visual. It could be as basic as using a map and compass to show when a person is lost, or a magnifying glass when someone's trying to find something.

Try using an image search for simple visual metaphors. For example, a search for 'decision' returns dice, question marks and people scratching their heads.

Bigger picture metaphors can also be a useful way to frame a landscape of information, particularly when sequences of interactions, relationships and dynamics are important parts of the content.

I find analogue metaphors resonate best – I've lost track of how many buckets, sieves and funnels I've drawn to show the narrowing of options, or to illustrate a consumer decision-making process.

Others I've seen successfully used are:

Board game, with items to collect, shortcuts and barriers along the way to an end goal.

Factory/machine, with pipes and valves, blockages and gauges showing system status.

Garden/growing, showing nurture, threats, progress, changing conditions, harvest.

GET VISUAL

2. Keep it simple

Prioritise crafting the message you need to convey over adding finesse. The sketchiest, hand-drawn stick figures and basic drawings can be as impactful as more polished versions. Like actors or props on a stage, your images are there to set a context and carry a message – a message we want people to respond to, understand and remember.

3. Arrows, your friends

Connection, tension, friction. Sequences, cycles and loop-backs. Arrows add the dynamic and flow a visual requires to guide your audience through the information, to highlight relationships, order and dependencies they need to understand.

4. Voice of the customer

Insights carry your own interpretation of the data and what it means, but be sure to use a selection of quotes in the visual to best represent the mindset or attitudes of the people you've met.

A good test of whether you've done this well is to strip out all the other layers of information and see whether it still holds up as a narrative without the supporting text. Beware, though, speech and thought bubbles are powerful magnets for attention, so use them wisely to get the message across, without making a graphic novel out of it.

5. Human scale

When it's time to print, every square-inch counts. A large visual provides a buffet of information seen by many people at once – a welcome departure from the one-print-per-person scenario. Going large also gets everyone out of their chairs, generating interaction and conversation. Ask your print shop how big you can go, and don't be shy.

6. Levels of zoom

A human-scale visual should work at two distances: across the room and at arms-length. Size your type and messages to invite or provoke from afar, then reward the viewer with depth and substance as they draw closer. You'll see this play out when you have two rows deep at your poster during a workshop. Use the 'squint test' to ensure the customer's voice and key points are readable from a couple of paces back.

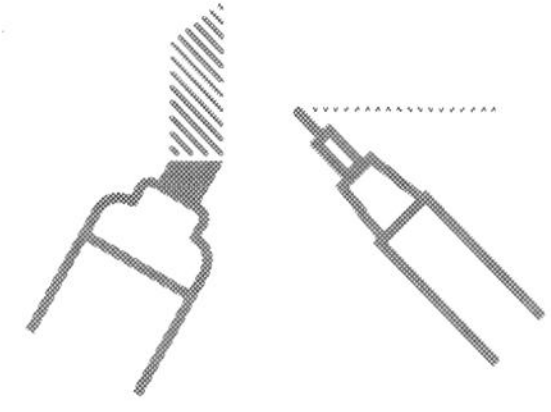

7. Fidelity

Different stages and types of project require different styles of visual, so aim for the appropriate level of detail and polish for the audience and the decisions they face at the time. Think: How long will the information remain relevant? How 'locked down' is the content? Do you want to convey definitive information or encourage interpretation and contribution? Knowing this should help you decide whether to stick with basic sketches, go digital with more finesse, or brief a graphic designer to make it sing.

8. Recycle

After a few of these visuals you'll have a library of commonly used figures, symbols and props to use in other artefacts. You'll always need to top up with bespoke items unique to each context, but this stash of usual suspects can save a lot of rework.

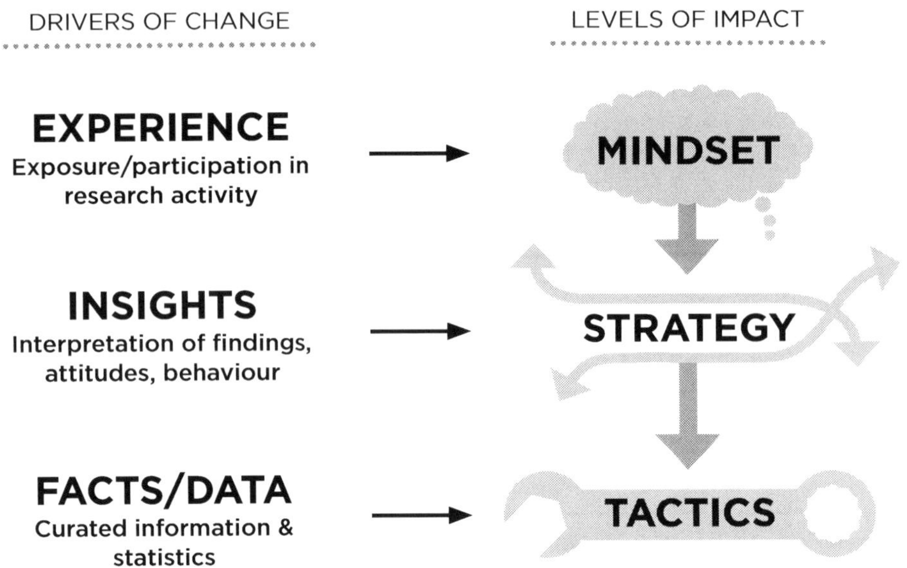

'You had to be there'

We've all told, or been told a 'location joke' - where it's only really funny to those who were there at the time - and where the nuance of a moment in context only has meaning to the person who experienced it.

Similarly, your success relies on your audience getting the punchlines - those moments which 'being there' enabled. Including team-members directly in the project goes a long way, but the nature of fieldwork makes 'change by experience' hard to scale to a larger group.

Your time in the field and through the depths of analysis gives you an experiential and informational advantage, providing a new lens through which to view things. This is the lens we want our clients or wider team to see through.

To counter this advantage, design experiences for people rather than presenting findings to them – staging immersive activities to bring a team closer to your journey of discovery – to frame their own insights and reach their own conclusions. This can have much more impact than a 'big reveal' of your findings.

Insight framing

My favourite approach to sharing research findings uses video, but transcripts or audio accompanied by photos can work, too.

You'll need:

- Videos/photos from fieldwork and a way to edit and share these to groups
- Flipchart-sized work-sheets and pens for note-taking
- (optional) a large format visual with your pre-distilled insights or themes mapped
- A curious team primed to participate

PREPARING YOUR MATERIALS

Dream team

Select a subset of participant profiles - people who bring to life the themes which emerged from the analysis - four to six participants is a good number. It will allow your group to split into two or three teams, each with two profiles to become familiar with.

Profile clips

Edit video footage from each of these sessions into around a 3–10-minute clip that offers a 'close encounter' with each participant.

Leave in those telling pauses, distant gazes, and interlace the clip with still photos of details, artefacts and context.

Trailer clip

Edit together a shorter 'mix-tape'-style trailer of highlights from all the profile clips.

Be creative with this edit. It's only a snapshot but should be enough to build intrigue, revealing contrasts in attitudes/behaviours between the individuals.

Worksheets

Use flipchart-sized note-taking templates for your team to capture observations. One sheet per profile. Each worksheet to include mugshot, context photos, demographics, life stage and background facts that won't necessarily come across in their video.

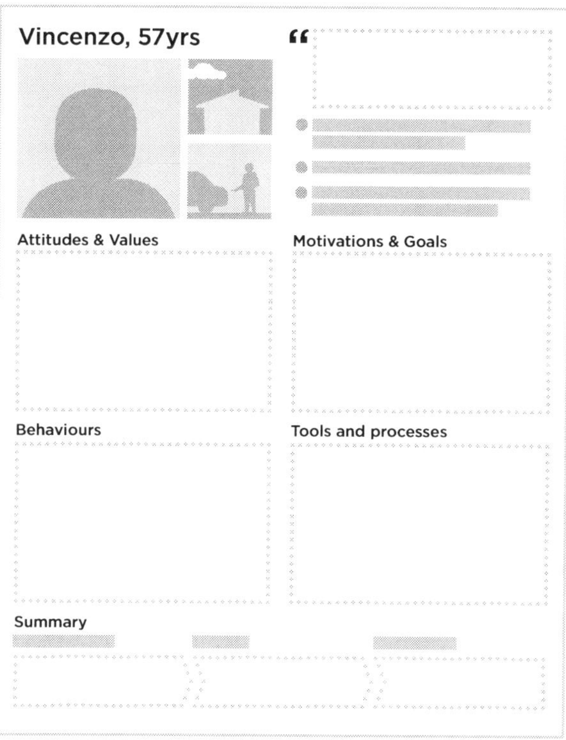

INSIGHT FRAMING

Leave blank sections to note down attitudes, behaviours, motivations, favourite tools, a 'killer quote' etc. A simple 'what did they say, do, think, feel?' map might suffice, but it's worth using targeted prompts specific to answering the 'unknowns' in the project objectives, to tease out insights rather than just general observations.

Create room for a summary of insights. Provide scaffolding, such as: Type of customer:_____ needs:_____, so she can:_____, because:_____

This provides focus for the team to agree on what's really going on in this customer's world, articulating the user's unique goals, needs and motivations.

These summaries are perfect starting points for 'How might we ...?' idea-generating sessions.

FACILITATING THE SESSION

Let's say you have twelve in your stakeholder group and you're ready with:

- your 'Trailer' clip, including all profiles
- six 'profile' video clips
- six worksheets, one for each profile
- optional large visual/map
- a common room with a large screen
- two quiet breakout spaces

1. Prime the team

Outline the activities so the group knows what to expect and what's expected of them. Hand out sticky notes/pens and ask them to take a handful of notes during the video. Turn up the volume on the trailer clip and hit play.

2. Take the temperature

After the trailer ... shut up. Rather than asking 'So, what did you notice?' or worse: 'Did you notice how ...?' just zip it, and let the group share their responses and observations.

They've only seen the tip of the iceberg but their reactions will reveal bias and assumptions, especially if you've pulled together polarising highlights. Hearing these (perhaps knee-jerk) thoughts will enable you to compare changes in viewpoints later – the measure you're looking for.

Don't let this conversation drag on, though. Move on to the individual profile videos before the team starts drawing tempting conclusions.

3. Split it and hit it

Break the group into three teams, giving each team two profile clips to watch. Select pairs of profiles to reveal contrast: a rejecter with an advocate; a dabbler with an enthusiast, so each team will take this deeper dive. Then provide the worksheets for each profile.

4. Share & compare

Once the teams have reached a better understanding of their two individuals and have generated their own insights in response, reconnect back as a group to share their work sheets and summaries, one profile at a time.

Encourage or raise questions to reveal aspects unique to each customer. Adding your or their anecdotes from the field can correct assumptions or add context not available through the clip.

5. Synthesis

Before the conversation starts to fragment, ask each group member to commit to a shortlist of personal reflections – a 'top five' insights – challenges, opportunities, or whatever gets closer to moving the conversation forward. Each item on a sticky note.

This is where a wall-sized poster comes into its own. Just make sure it's human scale (go large). Think of this as scaffolding for the team's own insights. It might be stages in a customer's journey or a loose group of broadly titled themes: drivers, barriers, influences, etc.

Pin up the large-scale visual or map of your key themes with enough space for the whole group to gather in front of it. Each could take turns to approach the poster, reading their stickies aloud and placing them to the part of the map they best fit.

If you don't have a visual, start with a blank wall and guide the teams through a grouping/theme exercise to summarise their insights.

TERRY
Attitudes + Values
Summary

INSIGHT FRAMING

WHY DOES THIS WORK?

During the trailer clip, responses can be knee-jerk but bring bias and assumptions to the surface. Everyone in the group receives the same snapshot of all six individuals, and they develop a curiosity for the full story. Maybe there's one they align with, personally, and one or two which will test their ideas of what a 'typical' customer is.

Then the profile clips provide each team the experience of getting to know two contrasting characters at a deeper level. Together they build a profile of their attributes defining what matters to them and their needs.

Going deep with just two of the people makes them realise there must be also more to the other four than they initially saw.

During share & compare, summaries and questions are asked and comparisons made as the profiles are being presented back to the group:

'Did you find out why she went to so much effort to do X?'

'Nikki did that, too, but she did it because ...'

'Our guy didn't bother with any of that because he ...'

During synthesis, as team members' thoughts land around themes, you'll witness an echo (and variations) of your own insights, but this time in their language with the weight of their priorities behind them.

The team becomes invested in the output because it's aligned with, and supported by, their thoughts. It feels like the experience has changed them, as it did you.

From here it's a matter of maintaining momentum.

Momentum

EMPATHY, DISCOVERY, OBSERVATION, RESEARCH, UNDERSTANDING, IDENTIFICATION, INTERPRETATION, SYNTHESIS, DEFINITION.

If you've been following one of the dozens of hypothetical design-process diagrams, you'll realise you're at a transition – you can probably tick off any of these first phases.

From here the activity changes into something more generative. Less research, more design.

Having taken your client team through the what, who and why ... they've realised and taken onboard the 'so what?'

Now it's time for the 'now what?'

(And maybe some 'how might we ...?' if that's the way you like to frame your design challenges).

Keeping the customer in mind

The most validating and high-five-worthy outcome of a fieldwork study is a team acting in response to the insights, opportunities or challenges as they launch into idea-generating mode. This means shaping potential solutions to the (now well-defined) needs of their customer.

It's a comforting thought that your team has the customer in mind, but sometimes a nudge is required to ensure solutions stay relevant to the user and their context.

It's your responsibility to be that nudge; to cut to how the product or service is experienced by the customer.

Principles

Guide your team through an exercise where you define guiding aspirational principles for the product or service experience.

Principles tell a design team what their solution must embody, express or achieve for the customer in order to offer a great experience, e.g. 'We've done all the thinking so the user doesn't have to', or 'It's always obvious to the user where they are, and what's next in the process.

They provide a great stepping stone between the insights gained and the next steps of prototyping.

What should the product enable? How should the product behave? How should the customer feel during or after interacting with the product?

Well-defined principles will be evergreen and help keep the voice of the customer in the design conversation, so display them prominently in a common workspace to act as a sense-checker for design decisions.

Prototypes

Building physical, tangible versions of design solutions brings hypotheses to life, introducing great opportunities to critique and learn, especially from potential end-users of the product or service.

Even basic sketches or models of an idea can be used in a cycle of design, gain feedback and iterate. Encourage your team to follow this cycle. It's a well-worn road towards a successful product, and the best kind of momentum.

Exposing prototypes to potential customers during subsequent field research sessions provides an unbeatable feedback loop, particularly if you have a team member in-tow. But do reiterate to them, it's a time to learn from the participants' responses, not sell them on the idea.

Participation

Nothing builds and maintains momentum and appetite for field research like your client or team being part of it.

Time spent in context with customers is an investment which pays back in many ways: busted assumptions, silenced scepticism, increased ownership of outcomes, advocacy for both the customer and for themselves or others to be part of the next outing. Result.

Unless you want to become a customer tour guide, spending days on end in the field may not be practical for an entire team. Try spreading the note-taker role across a handful of colleagues one or two at a time. Yes, you'll lose the continuity a double-act of researcher and a single note-taker provides - and this is a tradeoff you'll need to manage and make clear - but this kind of exposure of team members to customers can do wonders for your project's impact and credibility.

As a rule of thumb I insist team members attend a minimum of two field visits to ensure they're not overly influenced by a single voice.

From doing for, to doing with ...

With a collaborative spirit, treating team members like equals and by drawing on your team's curiosity, it's possible to move from doing for, to doing with, providing mutually valuable participation in the field, then back in the war room.

... to helping become

With the right person, it's possible to move from doing with, to helping become. When the work ignites the right qualities in one of your team, operating as a player/coach, transitioning them into the driver's seat can quickly reach the point they're comfortable leading their own fieldwork. Another great result.

Mix it up

Complementing your fieldwork with other methods helps complete the picture of your customers' world, adding relevance and depth to your data, and your findings.

These three are my 'usual suspects':

Diary studies

Customers log their behaviours or interactions over time, as they progress towards a goal, or simply go about aspects of their lives you're interested in. For example, keeping a daily journal of spending to understand how people categorise their purchases.

Diary studies work well as a prelude to field visits, and should always include an exit interview. This is your opportunity to get to the 'why' as they elaborate on their diary entries. Diaries can be conducted with paper & pen, or using online tools like dscout.com.

Remote interviews

Interview a customer via phone or, ideally, video chat. These work well for hard-to-reach participants or for follow-up calls after a field visit.

Rapport is almost instant when you've previously met the participant, but requires extra charisma to build from scratch via video or phone.

Schedule a short chat in advance to get the introductions and any questions about the study out of the way. Fish for something going on in their day to enquire about at the beginning of the actual interview. 'So, have you dried out after that soaking from cycling home in the rain last week?'

Choose a platform which lets the person share their screen with you as they browse a website, conduct a task or show you through a gallery.

Metrics

Use surveys or other quantitative methods to back up your findings with numbers.

Make friends with analytics people in your organisation - those who monitor traffic or sales data for stores, sites. They can usually provide stats which reveal the extent or relevance of a finding to your customers, or provide clues for new areas of focus for your next field study.

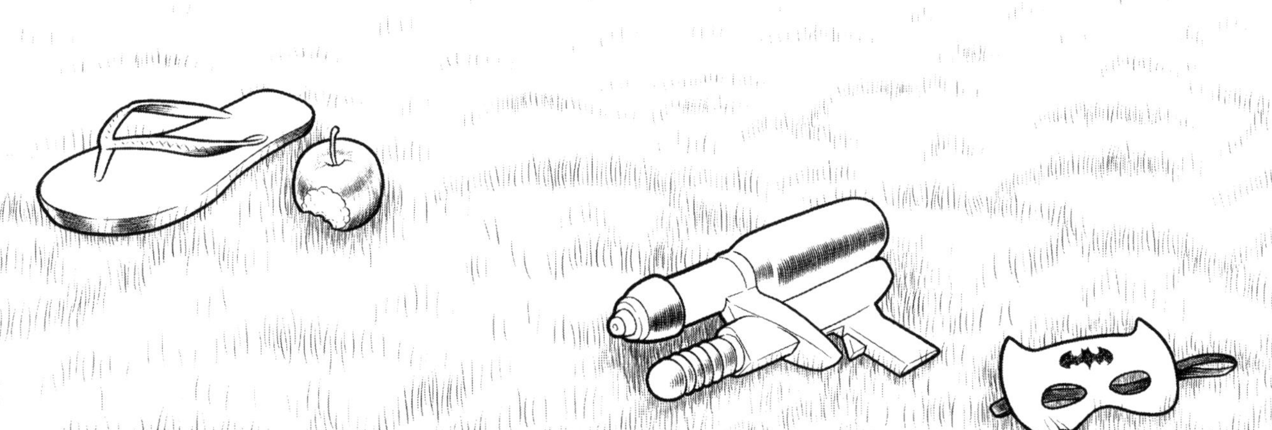

8. YOUR TURN

To bring, build, steal, share & care

Bring your own

Be creative. Let your experience and skills play into your research approach. Adapt and improve your work and bring your strengths. For example, if you're great with film, incorporate this medium into your projects. If you're a spreadsheet guru, try using this to sort your data. If you have a thing for theatre, try using actors to portray customers.

This works both ways - acknowledge where you need help and find people who can contribute in these areas.

Build your own

The difference between a good and a great researcher comes from qualities that can't be learned from a book:

CURIOSITY
INSTINCT
COMPOSURE
JUDGEMENT
COMMUNICATION

You'll need these in varying doses throughout a project, and the full set when you're with customers. Each project will stretch the qualities you already have and help you build on the others.

Steal

Researchers aren't alone in their pursuit to gain insight by studying or engaging with people. Steal from other professionals with a similar goal, be it an investigative reporter, anthropologist, journalist or detective. Drawing from their techniques will help you develop your own.

Share

As you gain confidence with an approach, share your experience with colleagues in an easy-to-digest format.

Packaging what you've learned in your own words forces you to be clear about the strengths, weaknesses and 'gotcha's' of an approach. Sharing it helps your colleagues understand how to best incorporate it in future work.

Care

The best outcomes from research come from teams who care - about the customer, organisation, product and process.

Genuinely caring - as you're planning, conducting, analysing and communicating your research - is the best head-start you can have when a design challenge lies ahead ...

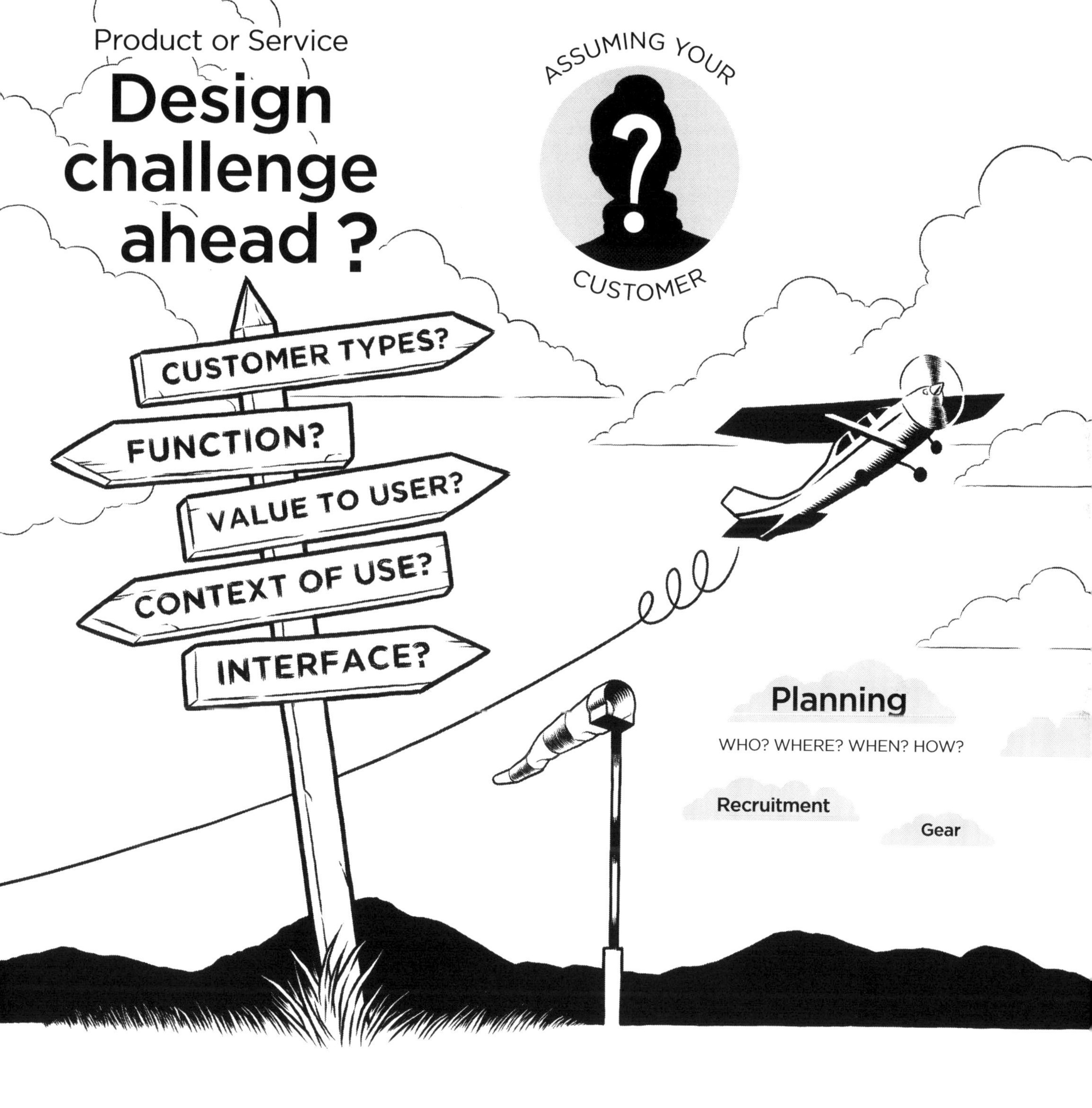
Product or Service
Design challenge ahead ?
ASSUMING YOUR
?
CUSTOMER
CUSTOMER TYPES?
FUNCTION?
VALUE TO USER?
CONTEXT OF USE?
INTERFACE?
Planning
WHO? WHERE? WHEN? HOW?
Recruitment
Gear

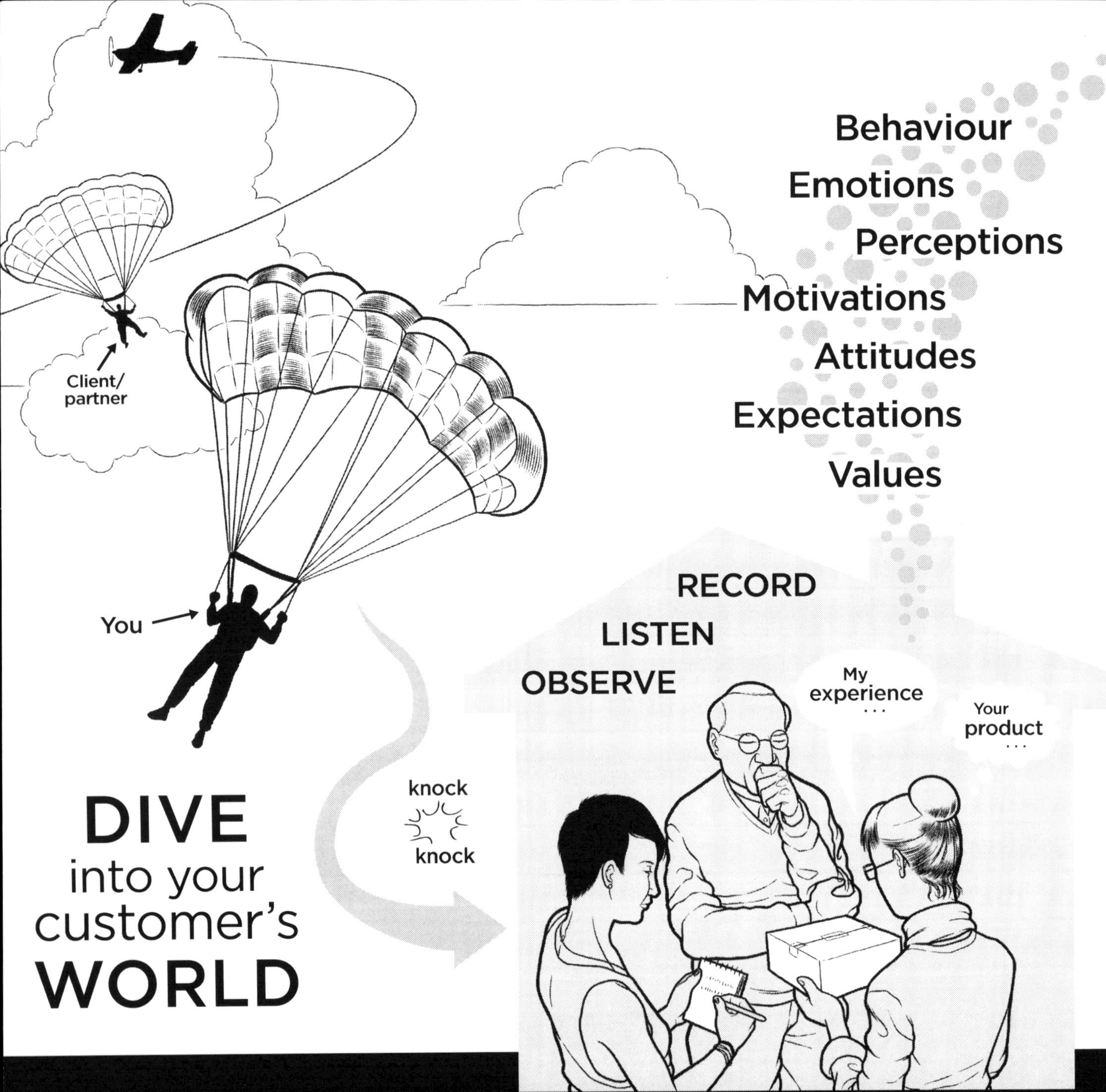
Behaviour
Emotions
Perceptions
Motivations
Attitudes
Expectations
Values
Client/
partner
You
RECORD
LISTEN
OBSERVE
My
experience
...
Your
product
...
knock
knock
DIVE
into your
customer's
WORLD

FINDINGS
ANALYSIS
EMPATHY
INSIGHTS
CURATION
Why?
What?
Who?
So
what?
PARTICIPATION
FACILITATION
Now
what?
Opportunities
Validation
Reality checks
Consensus
Confidence
INFORMED
DESIGN
DECISIONS
UNDERSTANDING
YOUR CUSTOMER
GREAT
CUSTOMER
EXPERIENCE
USERPALOOZA

Thank you

To the thousands of individuals who, by taking part in research, have allowed me into their lives, opened their homes and hearts and gifted me their stories. It's a privilege which never wears thin.

To the hundreds of clients, who have trusted me in my work.

To the dozens of colleagues, who have inspired and encouraged me to do, and be better.

Special thanks to Flow alumni in London and the Design & User Research Google group in San Francisco.

To Jude Watson, my editor, for paying as much attention to the details as the big picture.

To Mat Tait, my illustrator, for bringing life into these pages through great inking and thinking.

To my wife Jen, and daughter Georgie, for their patience, encouragement and creative input.

NICK BOWMAST

Design Researcher

Nick discovered the importance of understanding his own customers' needs in the early 1990s as a custom surfboard shaper. In this environment he learned the difference between what people say they want versus what they really need, and the value of working to a brief informed by reality.

His 25-year design career spans industrial, digital and architectural design. Research and design collided for Nick in London while working as a consultant for user experience and behavioural-research agencies.

Nick now works from New Zealand as an independent design researcher for local and international clients, applying his instinct for finding out what makes people tick to shape products, services, brands and environments both physical and digital.

bowmast.com

MAT TAIT

Illustrator

Mat is a New Zealand-based comics artist whose talent for visual storytelling was a perfect match for *USERPALOOZA*.

His award-winning work has been published widely, including in comics anthologies Kramer's Ergot and Comix2000 (L'Association), his visualised adaptation of Richard Wagner's opera *The Flying Dutchman*, for the Goethe Institut, and *The Heading Dog who Split in Half*, a book of illustrated New Zealand legends.

mattait.com

USERPALOOZA

All enquiries/bulk orders to nick@bowmast.com

www.userpalooza.co.nz

Printed in Poland
by Amazon Fulfillment
Poland Sp. z o.o., Wrocław